Easy Chairs
Hard Words

Conversations on the

Liberty of God

Douglas Wilson

Canon Press

MOSCOW, IDAHO

Douglas Wilson, *Easy Chairs, Hard Words: Conversations on the Liberty of God*

© 1991 by Douglas Wilson. Published by Canon Press, P.O. Box 8741, Moscow, ID 83843.

04 05 06   9 8 7 6 5

Cover design by Paige Atwood

Printed in the United States of America.

ISBN: 885767-30-7

ISBN-13: 978-1-885767-30-1
ISBN-10: 1-885767-30-7
Easy Chairs, Hard Words

Easy Chairs, Hard Words

Contents

Preface

I must confess that for many years I was prejudiced against the truths about grace contained in this small book, and taught against them with a sincerity common to the ignorant. But God is good; perhaps He will use this volume to undo some of the harm that I did. Although our God is almighty, and does as He pleases, the Scripture teaches us that He uses *means* to accomplish His purposes. It is consequently my prayer that He will use this book to lead more of His people out onto the ocean of His grace, until there is no land in sight.

The book is structured around a series of conversations between an older pastor, Martin Spenser, and a young man who has come to him for counsel. Although the truths contained in the conversations are biblical truths, the characters are entirely fictional, along with most of the incidents or events they relate. I have put these truths into a fictional setting merely to make them more readable, and hence more understandable.

I fear that the production of this book has placed me deeper in debt to quite a few people. My thanks go to those who read over the manuscript for me, making appropriate and helpful suggestions—Douglas Jones, Terry Morin, and my wife, Nancy. Of course any remaining problems are my responsibility. I am grateful to Tom Boyd for making it all possible, and to Mark and Chris LaMoreaux. All quotations from Scripture are from the New King James Version.

I offer this book to you with the hope that it will serve to advance the kingdom of God, and of His Christ. To the extent that the writing of any creature can, I pray that it will result in glory to God.

Introduction

I was brought up in a church which emphatically taught that a Christian could lose his salvation (there is no need to mention the denomination), so the doctrinal questions that assailed me now were uncomfortable, to say the least.

It would distress my parents grievously if I left the church, so I had never expressed my doubts to them. At the same time, I felt I needed to do something to answer the questions that came into my mind every time I opened my Bible. But how could I get answers without rocking the ecclesiastical boat?

One night after Sunday Service, when I couldn't get the message to even shake hands with the text, I was in a pretty desperate condition. There was a small church across town which I had sometimes heard contemptuously dismissed as "Calvinistic." I had always accepted that assessment, although I sometimes wondered what it meant. All I knew was that they believed Christians couldn't lose their salvation.

I looked up the name of the church in the yellow pages (there is no need to mention the denomination here either), and jotted down the name of the pastor. I looked at the clock and decided it wasn't too late to call, so I did.

I introduced myself, and said I had some pressing theological questions, and would he meet with me? His name was Martin Spenser, and he said he would be happy to. I explained my family situation to him, and told him that I was willing for the family to be disrupted over the "truth," but that I didn't want any commotion over my confusions and searching. He understood, and we set up an appointment for the next Wednesday.

One thing led to another, and the one meeting turned into a series of meetings. I had gone into the first meeting with a handful of basic, perplexing questions, and came away with a *truckload* of questions, and a buzzing head. It was apparent to both of us that we would have to meet many more times, which he quite pleasantly agreed to do.

As best as I can remember them, I have collected in this book our conversations. There has also been some reconstruction from my notes, as well as occasional lists of verses which I have also inserted. I hope the conversations are as edifying for you as they were for me.

_____ one _____

Can Salvation Be Lost?

Martin Spenser sat easily in a large chair next to the fireplace. We were in his study at home. After the usual exchange of pleasantries, I began the discussion. I still didn't know him very well at all, so I began somewhat nervously.

"Could you tell me how you became a Calvinist?"

He laughed and said, "Well, I didn't."

I must have looked baffled, so he went on.

"The term 'Calvinist' is really misleading. The issue for Christians should always be, 'What does the Bible say?' If the Bible teaches something, then it should be accepted as the biblical position. If the Bible does not, then it shouldn't be accepted at all."

"Then why do so many 'Calvinists' use the term?"

"Well, many biblical Christians use the term simply for the sake of convenience. It is for them a term of theological shorthand. They can let someone else know what their position is very quickly. Unfortunately, there are other Christians who adopt the term with the attitude forbidden by Paul—I am of Paul, I am of Apollos, and so forth."

"So why do you avoid the label?"

"I have found that it only works as a form of shorthand with people who are theologically educated, and it is frequently a problem even with them. With many people, I would have to say, 'I am a Calvinist, *but*. . . .'"

I must have still looked puzzled, because he went on.

"Look. The church you grew up in defines a Calvinist as anyone who believes in eternal security. But eternal security is only one tiny part of the teaching of what is called 'Calvinism.' There is no way that I could tell someone in that church that I am a Calvinist and be understood."

"So what label do you use?"

"I am a Christian. And the doctrines I hold are the doctrines of the Bible."

"But doesn't that sound arrogant? 'My position is the biblical position. What's *yours?*'"

"Yes, it can sound arrogant, and if I don't watch my heart constantly, it can actually be arrogant. But it appears to me to be what the Bible requires."

"What about the term 'Reformed'? I have heard some people use that before."

"It's better than 'Calvinist,' although I think the Bible discourages this kind of labeling at all. So I try not to use either. But I have had this opinion of labels for over twenty years, and people still insist on calling me a 'Calvinist,' and 'Reformed.' So if someone has to use something other than 'Christian,' I prefer to be called 'Reformed.' People don't understand that term either, but at least it doesn't carry a lot of negative baggage with it. They don't understand, but they don't *misunderstand* either."

"Okay," I said, getting to the question that was keeping me up nights. "Can a Christian lose his salvation?"

Martin didn't answer with a yes or a no. In fact, I was sort of surprised at how he began.

"I guess I have to ask *you* to define your terms. What do you mean by 'Christian,' and what do you mean by 'salvation'?"

I sat and thought a minute.

"A Christian is someone who has been born again, and has faith in Jesus Christ. Salvation is from sin and the consequences of sin. Someone loses his salvation when he foolishly rejects Christ, and falls back into the eternal consequences of that choice." I leaned back in my chair, feeling a little pleased with my definitions.

"And it bothers you to think that this sort of thing might happen?"

"Yes, it does. I know that in some places the Bible seems to teach that this can happen, but there are other passages which make it seem unthinkable."

"We'll look at some of those passages later. For now, let's continue with our definitions."

I nodded in agreement, so he went on.

"Suppose you saw a lifeguard rescuing a drowning person. The lifeguard was pulling the person in, and then for some reason the drowning man began to fight the lifeguard, pulled free, and went to the bottom."

"All right," I said.

"Did the drowning man lose his 'salvation'?"

"Well, yes."

"Really? Was he ever *saved*?"

"Okay, not in any ultimate way. True salvation would be the possession of those up on the beach."

"In other words, a man is only saved from something if that something doesn't happen to him, right? He is only saved from drowning if he doesn't drown?"

"Right."

"Now with regard to salvation from sin and hell, does God know which individuals will be 'up on the beach' eventually? Does He know who will wind up in heaven?"

"Certainly. God knows everything."

"So then, God sees who will possess this ultimate salvation?"

"Yes."

"Can this final salvation be lost?"

"Obviously not."

"So once you are *saved*, then you cannot lose it."

I nodded my head, wondering where this was taking me.

"So then, the disagreement between Christians is not over whether salvation can be lost. It is over whether a man in this life can know that *he will be saved.*"

I thought for a moment, and then agreed.

"Another way of putting this is to say that some Christians think that regeneration can be reversed, and other Christians do not. And that leads us to your definition of a Christian. You said that a Christian was someone who was born again through his faith in Jesus Christ, right?"

"Yes," I said.

"So his regeneration is dependent upon his faith?"

"Well, of course."

"But what if faith is dependent on regeneration?"

"What do you mean?"

"Suppose faith is a gift? And suppose further that the way God gives this gift is through regenerating a sinner's heart?"

"It is all very well to suppose. How do you know that it is? And if faith is a gift from God, then how is it genuinely *mine?*"

"There are two questions there. In order, we know that faith is a gift because the Bible says it is."

"Where?"

"Philippians 1:29. *For to you it has been granted on behalf of Christ, not only to believe in Him, but also to suffer for His sake.* This teaches that suffering for Christ is a gift, along with believing in Him. Both are gifts, and both are from God."

"Anywhere else?"

"Yes. Acts 18:27. In talking about the ministry of Apollos, Luke tells us that he was a great help to *those who had believed through grace.* It doesn't say that they believed in grace, but rather through grace. Grace enabled them to believe. So again, faith, or belief, is a gift."

This was all pretty strange to me, so I asked for another passage.

"Well, this one is disputed, but it is worth noting. Ephesians 2:8-9. *For by grace you have been saved through faith, and that not of yourselves; it is the gift of God, not of works, lest anyone should boast.*"

"What is the dispute over?"

"It is over the referent of *that*. What is the gift of God? Salvation? Grace? Faith? A plain reading of it in English would indicate that you have been saved by grace, through faith, and that faith was not from yourself, but was a gift from God. The fact that faith is a gift keeps anyone from boasting."

"You said English. What about Greek?"

"That is where there is some dispute. Some have argued that *faith* cannot be the referent of *that* because in Greek the noun *faith* is feminine, while the pronoun for *that* is neuter."

"Well, doesn't that settle it? Doesn't the pronoun have to match the noun in gender? I don't know much Greek, but. . . ."

"No, it doesn't have to match. With concrete nouns, like *house*, or *ship*, it usually will match. But abstract nouns like *faith*, *hope* and *charity* take the neuter. Thus, there is no reason in the Greek grammar of the passage to reject the plain reading of the text. Faith is a gift."

"You said there were two questions I had raised."

"Yes. You asked how faith could be *mine* if it were a gift."

"Oh, right," I said.

"You are concerned that if faith is a gift from God, then my faith in Him is really an optical illusion; it *looks* like I am exercising faith, but it is really He who does it?"

"Yes. That's exactly it. It makes the whole thing seem like a charade."

"Do you mind a physical example?"

"Not if it helps."

"When a young man hits adolesence, does he find himself, all of a sudden, with sexual desire?"

"Well, of course."

"Is the desire *his*?"

I answered carefully. "He experiences it. It sure isn't somebody else's desire."

"Prior to this, had he by an act of the will commanded his body to change?"

"No. It just happens."

"So his body is filled with testosterone, and his mind with desire."

"Right."

"And it is *his* desire?"

"Yes."

"But who made the body this way?"

"God."

"So this body, and the bodily desire he has, are *gifts?* From God?"

"Yes."

"And the desire is nevertheless *his,* and he is responsible for how he acts, based on those desires?"

"I guess so."

"So why do we have a double standard? If God can give physical gifts this way, why do we say He cannot give faith? It is the same sort of thing. He gives me a new heart, and this new heart believes in Him. And I am the one believing."

I thought I almost had it, so I said, "Could you say it briefly another way?"

"Sure. I have faith in God because He gave it to *me.* Of course it is mine. He gave it to me."

I grinned. "I see. Suppose someone told me that a birthday present wasn't mine because it was given to me. That's not an argument against my possession of it. It is mine *because* it was a gift."

"Right. And the fact that we are dealing with faith doesn't change things at all."

"Okay. Now how did we get here? We were talking about whether Christians can lose their salvation."

"It all ties in. If my salvation is something God does in me, through me, and for me, then He will not cease doing it. If I am saved through faith, and I am, and faith is a gift, and it is, then that faith will not falter. It is the work of God."

"I see."

"But if I am saved by faith, and faith is the work of man, then I have every right to be insecure. I may in fact be lost."

I nodded my head, and got up to go. "Thank you very

much. I am afraid that's more than enough to chew on. May I see you next week?"

"Next week."

— two —

— two —

Can Christ Lose a Christian?

"Do you mind if we go over something again? I think we need to talk a little more about whether we can lose our salvation."

Martin laughed. "Sure. But there would be a lot more peace in the church if Christians learned to frame such questions more biblically."

"How do you mean?"

"When the question is posed as to whether a Christian can lose his salvation, those for and against line up, and debate the question *as it was posed*. But salvation is not a personal possession of ours, like car keys, which can be misplaced by us."

"So what is the real question?"

"The way the question is usually asked, we wonder if a Christian can lose his salvation, which is the same as asking whether a Christian can lose Christ. Some say yes, and others no."

"And you would say. . . ?"

"I would ask whether Christ can lose a Christian."

"I don't get you."

"Christians are those who are redeemed or *purchased* for God through the blood of Christ. We have been bought with a price. Now if someone, so purchased, winds up in Hell, then *who* has lost that person's salvation?"

"I'm sorry, I must be thick. I still don't get what you are driving at."

"Christians cannot lose their salvation, for the simple reason that their salvation does not belong to them. It belongs to Christ. If anyone is to lose it, it must be He. And He has promised not to."

"Where does the Bible teach that we are His possession?"

"There are many passages which cover this—too many to cover tonight. Why don't we just look at a few? I'll give you a list of others."

"Fair enough."

"In Revelation 5:9-10, the new song in honor of the Lamb states that He has redeemed us to God by His blood from every tribe, tongue, people, and nation."

"And. . . ."

"In 1 Corinthians 6:20, it says, *For you were bought at a price; therefore glorify God in your body and in your spirit, which are God's.*"

"It seems pretty clear."

"Right. In salvation, Christ does not become our property; we become His. So in discussing this, we must remember that all the saving is done by Him. Those who want to maintain that salvation can be lost are really saying that *He* is the one who loses it."

"This throws the whole debate into a completely different light."

"It does. And frankly, it is the difference between grace and works."

"How so?"

"To assert that a man can lose his salvation through what he does or does not do is to assert, in the final analysis, salvation by works."

"But the church in which I grew up taught that you can lose your salvation, but they also preached salvation by grace."

"Not quite. They preached a conversion experience by grace. But how is that experience to be maintained and protected? And by whom? They begin with the Spirit, but seek to finish through human effort."

I must have looked confused, so he continued.

"Were you ever taught that you could, by committing certain sins, place yourself outside of Christ?"

"Yes, and it terrified me."

"Now, let's say that you committed such a sin, and then were killed in a car wreck? Where would you go?"

"To Hell."

"And why?"

"Because I had sinned, and a holy God cannot look on sin."

"And your salvation, or lack of it, was up to whom?"

"You are arguing that it was up to me. I can tell you that it certainly *felt* that way. The more I wanted to serve God, the more condemned I felt."

"Don't you see that your insecurity was the result of your salvation riding on a roulette wheel every day?"

"How so?"

"If you died on Monday, you go to be with the Lord. If you died on Thursday, off to Hell. On Sunday night, you are heaven-bound again."

"You are saying that this is salvation by works?"

"What else can we call it? And it produces two kinds of people. One group is confident in their own righteousness, but they have watered down the righteous standards of God in order to delude themselves this way. The other group is comprised of sincere people, who, because they are honest, realize that they are under condemnation."

"It seems a little strong to say that they are professing salvation by works, though."

"Paul rebuked Peter to his face at Antioch, and why? Because Peter did something as *trivial* as withdrawing table fellowship from Gentiles temporarily. But Paul knew that the gospel was threatened by this. How much more is it threatened through teaching that a Christian can do a 'work' which will blow his salvation away? This teaching makes salvation depend upon the works of men."

"You contrasted this with grace."

"Correct. Salvation by grace is a gift from God. Salvation by works is man's attempt to earn his way into the presence of God, or in this case, his attempt to earn his right to stay there."

"But what is to prevent someone from saying they are saved by grace, and then going to sin up a storm?"

Martin laughed. "Nothing at all. Sinners can say and do what they please. Until the judgment."

"But how would you answer the objection?"

"There are two things worth noting about it. One is that having to answer it places me in good company. The apostle Paul had to answer the same obejction in Romans 6, against those who objected to *his* message of grace. Secondly, the answer is the one Paul gives in that passage. Recipients of grace do not get to decide to receive *forgiveness grace,* while refusing *death-to-sin grace.* How can we who died to sin, still live in it?"

"But aren't there some who teach that salvation can be lost simply to keep this type of person from presumption?"

"Out of a concern for 'holiness,' there have been some who insist on teaching that Christians can lose their salvation. They say that without this perspective, people will abuse grace. But if you hold the biblical perspective, you do not consider grace a possession of your own that can be abused. Rather, grace belongs to *God,* and He never abuses it."

"Keep going."

"In Ephesians 2:8-9, we learn that we are saved by grace through faith. In the next verse, we learn that we are *God's workmanship,* created in Christ Jesus for *good works* prepared beforehand by God. God's grace is never truly abused because it belongs to *God.* Outsiders abuse the word *grace,* but they cannot touch the thing itself."

"You sound like you have very little respect for those on the other side of this issue."

"That is not quite true. Some of them are teaching another gospel, and the condemnation of the apostle is sufficient for them. But there are others who are true Christians, and who hold this position because of their reading of certain texts. Hebrews 10:26 is a good example."

"You respect them?"

"Yes. I believe them to be wrong, but their error proceeds from a desire to be honest with the text. With the purveyors of a false gospel, the error comes from an almost complete confusion of grace and works."

"What about Hebrews 10:26?"

"We are almost out of time. Why don't I read that passage, adding some comments of my own based on the context of Hebrews. Then you can go back through the book with that context in mind. It should be helpful in chapter six as well."

"Fine."

"For if we sin willfully *by going back to the sacrifices of bulls and goats* after we have received the knowledge of the truth *that Christ was the once for all sacrifice for sin*, there no longer remains a sacrifice for sins *because temple sacrifice of bulls and goats is a system that is fading away*, but a certain fearful expectation of judgment, and fiery indignation which will devour the adversaries *because they are sacrificing their bulls and goats in a temple that will be destroyed in just a few years*."

I laughed. "Is all that in the Greek?"

Martin grinned. "No, but it is in the context. Read through the book of Hebrews with the impending destruction of Jerusalem in mind, and consider the problem caused by professing Christians who were being tempted to return to Jerusalem in order to sacrifice there. The fire that was going to consume the enemies of God in this passage is *not* hellfire."

"So what is the basic issue here?"

"It is grace—grace and works. Works is a barren mother; she will never have any children, much less gracious children. Grace is fruitful; her children are many, and they all work hard."

Texts on the Preservation of the Saints

Isaiah 54:10
"For the mountains shall depart and the hills be removed, but *My kindness shall not depart from you,* nor shall My covenant of peace be removed," says the Lord, who has mercy on you.

Jeremiah 32:40
And I will make *an everlasting covenant* with them, that I will not turn away from doing them good; but I will put My fear in their hearts *so that they will not depart from Me.*

Matthew 18:14
Even so it is *not* the will of your Father who is in heaven *that one of these little ones should perish.*

John 3:16
For God so loved the world that He gave His only begotten Son, that whoever believes in Him *should not perish* but have everlasting life.

John 3:36
He who believes in the Son *has everlasting life*; and he who does not believe the Son shall not see life, but the wrath of God abides on him.

John 5:24
Most assuredly, I say to you, he who hears My word and believes in Him who sent Me has everlasting life, *and shall not come into judgment,* but has passed from death into life.

John 6:35
And Jesus said to them, "I am the bread of life. He who comes to Me *shall never hunger,* and he who believes in *Me shall never thirst.*"

John 6:37

All that the Father gives Me will come to Me, and the one who comes to Me *I will by no means cast out.*

John 6:40

And this is the will of Him who sent Me, that of all He has given Me *I should lose nothing,* but should raise it up at the last day.

John 6:47

Most assuredly, I say to you, he who believes in Me *has everlasting life.*

John 10:27-29

My sheep hear My voice, and I know them, and they follow Me. And I give them eternal life, and *they shall never perish;* neither shall *anyone* snatch them out of My hand. My Father, who has given them to Me, is greater than all; and no *one* is able to snatch them out of My Father's hand.

Romans 5:8-10

But God demonstrates His own love toward us, in that while we were still sinners, Christ died for us. *Much more then,* having now been justified by His blood, *we shall be saved from wrath through Him.* For if when we were enemies we were reconciled to God through the death of His Son, much more, having been reconciled, *we shall be saved* by His life.

Romans 8:1

There is therefore now *no condemnation* to those who are in Christ Jesus, who do not walk according to the flesh, but according to the Spirit.

Romans 8:29

For whom He foreknew, He also *predestined to be conformed* to the image of His Son, that He might be the firstborn among many brethren.

Romans 8:34-39

Who is he who condemns? It is Christ who died, and furthermore is also risen, who is even at the right hand of God, who also *makes intercession for us. Who shall separate us from the love of Christ?* Shall tribulation, or distress, or persecution, or famine, or nakedness, or peril, or sword?

As it is written: "For Your sake we are killed all day long; We are accounted as sheep for the slaughter."

Yet in all things we are more than conquerors through Him who loved us. For I am persuaded that neither death nor life, nor angels nor principalities nor powers, nor things present nor things to come, nor height nor depth, nor any other created thing, *shall be able to separate us* from the love of God which is *in Christ Jesus* our Lord.

1 Corinthians 1:8-9

Who will also confirm you *to the end,* that you may be *blameless* in the day of our Lord Jesus Christ. God is faithful, by whom you were called into the fellowship of His Son, Jesus Christ our Lord.

2 Corinthians 4:14

Knowing that He who raised up the Lord Jesus will *also raise us up* with Jesus, and will present us with you.

2 Corinthians 5:5

Now He who has prepared us for this very thing is God, who also *has given us the Spirit as a guarantee.*

Ephesians 1:5

Having predestined us to adoption as sons by Jesus Christ to Himself, according to the good pleasure of His will.

Ephesians 1:13-14

In Him you also trusted, after you heard the word of truth, the gospel of your salvation; in whom also, having believed, you were *sealed* with the Holy Spirit of promise, who is *the guarantee of our inheritance* until the redemption of the purchased possession, to the praise of His glory.

Ephesians 4:30
And do not grieve the Holy Spirit of God, by whom you were *sealed* for the day of redemption.

1 Thessalonians 5:23-24
Now may the God of peace Himself, sanctify you completely; and may your whole spirit, soul, and body *be preserved blameless* at the coming of our Lord Jesus Christ. He who calls you is faithful, who also will do it.

2 Timothy 4:18
And the Lord will deliver me from every evil work *and preserve me* for His heavenly kingdom. To Him be glory forever and ever. Amen!

Hebrews 9:12
Not with the blood of bulls and calves, but with His own blood He entered the Most Holy Place once for all, having obtained *eternal redemption.*

Hebrews 9:15
And for this reason He is the Mediator of the new covenant, by means of death, for the redemption of the transgressions under the first covenant, that those who are called may receive the promise of the *eternal inheritance.*

Hebrews 10:14
For by one offering He has *perfected forever* those who are being sanctified.

1 Peter 1:5
Who are *kept by the power of God* through faith for salvation ready to be revealed in the last time.

1 John 2:19

They went out from us, but they were not of us; for if they had been of us, they would have continued with us; but they went out that they might be made manifest, that none of them were of us.

1 John 2:25

And this is the *promise* that He has promised us—eternal life.

2 John 5:11-13

And this is the testimony: that God has given us *eternal life,* and this life is in His Son. He who has the Son has life; he who does not have the Son of God does not have life. These things I have written to you who believe in the name of the Son of God, that you may *know* that you have eternal life, and that you may continue to believe in the name of the Son of God.

Jude 24-25

Now to Him who is able to *keep you from stumbling, and to present you faultless* before the presence of His glory with exceeding joy, To God our Savior, Who alone is wise, be glory and majesty, dominion and power, both now and forever. Amen.

_____ three _____

Ideas Have Consequences

"What difference does it all make?" I asked.

Martin took a sip of his coffee, and answered the question with a question.

"What kind of difference do you mean? For the individual Christian, or for the Church, or both?"

"Well, I first came to visit you because the difference it makes to me was obvious. The doctrine I held before did little more than torment me. I was constantly in fear over the possibility of losing my salvation."

"But. . . ?"

"But I have friends who hold to those same doctrines with enthusiastic cheerfulness. Are these teachings something which _I_ needed to hear for _my_ Christian life, but which are not necessary for the Church at large?"

Martin nodded. "I see what you are asking. Even if all this is true, is it something the Church needs to believe? Is the Church hindered in her work if these doctrines are neglected or rejected?"

"Right. If _some_ Christians seem to get along just fine without it, why can't the Church as a whole?"

"Because ideas have consequences, and because the Church is made up of individuals."

"Okay. Explain."

"Ideas have consequences, not because each individual

27

is consistent, but because groups of people are consistent *over time.*"

"What do you mean by that?"

"Let's take a clear example from outside the faith. Have you ever known an atheist who was a decent, law-abiding citizen?"

I nodded. "Yes."

"Now was he being consistent with the basic premises of his atheistic worldview?"

I laughed. "No. And we had many discussions about it. He treated me with respect, but given his worldview, I was nothing more than a mass of protoplasm."

Martin continued, "Now my point is this: Individual atheists can frequently be inconsistent, but *atheistic societies never are.*"

"Never are inconsistent, you mean?"

"Right. Over time, the beliefs of individuals will be consistently applied by the group, even if many of the individuals who brought this about did not apply them. Atheists can function in free societies, but atheists do not *establish* free societies. They establish societies which are hellholes."

"Apply this to the Church, then."

"The basic issue we have been discussing these past couple weeks has been the difference between man-centered religion, and God-centered religion."

"I follow that."

"Now, have you ever known any Christian whose beliefs, or doctrines, were what we have been calling 'man-centered,' but whose life was clearly God-centered?"

I nodded again. "Yes."

"And we would call that inconsistent?"

"Yes."

"And if you wind up changing churches, you will very quickly encounter Christians whose doctrines are 'God-centered,' but whose lives are man-centered. This is also inconsistent."

"Well, this brings us back to my first question. If this is

the case, what difference does it all make?"

"It is quite simple. The Church, being an assembly of people, will eventually live in a manner consistent with her doctrine *over time*. If the doctrine is man-centered, then there will come a time when the lifestyle, morals, ceremonies, teaching, *etcetera*, are also man-centered."

"So even though an individual is inconsistent with his false doctrine, the Church at large will eventually be consistent with it."

"Correct. This explains why certain beliefs can be held by pious Christians, while those same beliefs go on to corrupt and defile the piety of the Church."

"Can you give me an example from church history?"

"Certainly. Consider *revival*. What does that term mean?"

I grinned. "A week of nightly meetings?"

"That is what it has come to mean. Arrange for a speaker, print the flyers, gather the troops, and work up a revival. From start to finish, it is the work of man."

"What did revival mean before?"

"It referred to a time when the sovereign Holy Spirit moved in a congregation in such a way as to reveal the glory of Jesus Christ. From start to finish, *it was the work of God*."

"What is a true revival like?"

"I don't know," he said. "All the knowledge of true revival today is secondhand—through books. The last healthy revival was in the mid-nineteenth century."

"What happened?"

"Revival, which is a gift of God, has been turned into a work of man through theological confusion. The result is *revivalism*, not revival."

"What is the difference?"

"Well, there are two kinds of revivalism. One is where a denomination has a long tradition of having these meetings, everyone is used to it, they go and listen, and then go home. It is little more than a religious seminar. And, as seminars go, some of them might be worthwhile."

"And the other?"

"The other is the result of taking the whole idea of re-vival more seriously. The people expect fireworks, so they see to it that there are fireworks. It is nothing more than reli-gious enthusiasm and fanaticism."

"But weren't some of the great revival preachers of the past—men you respect—accused of religious fanaticism too?"

"They certainly were. And if God is merciful to us and sends true revival again, the charges of fanaticism will be heard again."

"But. . . ."

"I know. Couldn't a Christian make the point that the whole distinction between revival and revivalism is a false one, and that all such events are fanatical to some degree or another?"

"Right."

Martin nodded. "It is a legitimate concern. First, can we agree that there is such a thing as true fanaticism?"

"Sure. I don't believe anyone would disagree there. Re-ligious fanatics have always been around."

"Now, the next question is this: Does the Bible teach anything which, if applied, would result in the one applying it to be accused of fanaticism?"

I smiled. "You tell me."

"How about 1 Peter 1:8? 'Though now you do not see Him, yet believing, you rejoice with *joy inexpressible and full of glory.*' Or Ephesians 3:17-19? 'That you . . . may be able to comprehend with all the saints what is the width and length and depth and height—*to know the love of Christ which passes knowledge.*' I don't know. A little extreme, don't you think?"

I sat for a moment, thinking. Martin spoke again.

"Christians get used to such passages. There it is, safe on the page. But there is no way for a Christian to be filled with inexpressible joy without it affecting his demeanor and behavior. And when it does, he will be accused of fanati-cism. Many Christians, in their concern over religious fa-naticism, have gotten rid of not only the fanaticism, but also the religion."

"So what are the characteristics of true revival, over against revivalism?"

"We have been talking about God-centeredness versus man-centeredness. The distinction follows us into our discussion of the criteria by which *everything* is to be evaluated; teaching and lifestyle, or, put another way, doctrine and morals."

"Okay. Let's start with doctrine."

"In a true revival, doctrine is the emphasis, and the doctrine is God-centered. In revivalism, because man is the center, feelings are emphasized. In revival, truth overwhelms the mind, resulting in an emotional response—inexpressible joy. In revivalism, the emotions are excited directly, and any number of teachings, true or false, can do *that*."

"What about morality?"

"In a true revival, the change in the moral behavior of those blessed is significant and lasting. With revivalism, very little is done to teach the people to restrain their passions. In fact, because the 'revival' encourages a lack of restraint in the church, it is not long before a lack of restraint is evident elsewhere, usually in the area of sexual morality."

"Are you saying that in order to have a true revival, a belief in God's exhaustive sovereignty is necessary?"

"Yes."

"But didn't men like Charles Finney deny this particular truth? And wasn't he part of the revivals of the nineteenth century?"

"Yes, he did deny it, and he was certainly a participant in 'revivals.' But he was one of those who effectively introduced the man-centered doctrines and practices which were the death of true revivals in this country."

"You know," I said, "I thought I had gotten used to the strange things you say from time to time. But this takes the cake! I have some friends who are really into revival, and they read books by Finney all the time."

Martin was shaking his head. "I know, I know. It is ironic. When Christians periodically despair of the current state of the church, and come to think, correctly, that the only thing which will help us is revival, they then turn to one of the men who was a major part of the problem."

"So how would you summarize all this?"

"I would say that God is over all, and through all, and in all. Anyone who denies this, in any measure, is a hindrance to true heaven-sent revival."

_____ four _____

Carnal Reasoning

Martin shifted easily in his seat while I carefully thought over my next question.

"Some of my friends at my church have figured out that I have been coming to see you," I said.

Martin nodded, and waited.

"Naturally," I said, "they are somewhat concerned."

"Naturally. About what?"

"Well, they say that Christians who believe in the exhaustive sovereignty of God are setting themselves up."

"For. . . ?"

"For the temptation which says that because God controls everything, then the way I live doesn't really matter."

"I see. In other words, if I am elect, then my sins won't damn me, and if I am not, then all the good works in the world won't save me. Is that it?"

"Yes. That is exactly it. If the whole thing was settled before the world began, then why bother? My friends know that there are true Christians who believe this, but they think that, because of this theology, these Christians will tend to become careless about how they live."

"Why should we take responsibility for our actions after we have embraced a theology which cuts the nerve of personal responsibility?"

"Right. If God controls everything, then what room is there for personal holiness?"

Martin thought for a moment. "The problem is not with your friends' concern for personal holiness. That is admirable. All Christians should set their faces against carnal living on the part of professing Christians. But it does no good to oppose carnal living with carnal reasoning."

"What do you mean?"

"When someone is whooping it up down at the bars, or sleeping with his girlfriend, why do we say it is sin?"

"Is this a trick question?"

Martin laughed. "You might say that. Why do we call such things sin?"

"Because the Bible does."

"Exactly. So this carnal living we have been talking about is a lifestyle that is not in submission to the clear teaching of the Word of God."

"Well, sure. But I still don't see where you are going with this."

"Now if carnal living is a lifestyle that does not submit to God's Word, then how should we define carnal reasoning?"

"The same way, I suppose?"

"Right. It is not enough to submit what we do externally to God; we must also submit *the way we think*. Your friends are trying to defend God's standards for living by abandoning His standards for thinking. It cannot be successful."

"Is there a passage where this point is clear?"

"Yes, in Philippians. Chapter 2, verses 12 and 13."

I turned to Philippians and read. *Therefore, my beloved, as you have always obeyed, not as in my presence only, but now much more in my absence, work out your own salvation with fear and trembling; for it is God who works in you both to will and to do for His good pleasure.* I looked up.

"What does the passage say God is doing?" Martin asked.

I looked down at my Bible again. "It says that He is working in the Philippians, both in willing and doing, and that the result is His good pleasure."

"And what would carnal reasoning do with that?"

"Well, the response would be that if God is doing the

willing, and if God is doing the doing, and the result is what-ever He wants, then there is no reason for me to put myself out. It is going to happen anyway."

"Right. The reasoning says that if God is going to do the work, then why should I have to?"

I nodded, and Martin went on.

"But what application of this truth does Paul command the Philippians to obey?"

I looked at the passage again. "He tells *them* to work out their own salvation, with fear and trembling." I glanced down further. "And in the next verse he goes on to specific ethical instruction—to avoid murmuring and disputing."

I sat and thought for a moment. "But my friends would say that the application they are making is obvious—common sense."

"Well, it certainly is common. But is it biblical?"

"Why do so many Christians fall for this line of reason-ing then? It seems like a trap that is extremely easy to fall into."

"Well, yes, it is easy to fall into. But it is also easy to drink too much, not watch your tongue, lust after women, and so forth. And *these* are things which the church recog-nizes as sin, and warns the people against. But carnal reason-ing is also easy, and almost no one warns the people."

"Why not?"

"Sheep are hungry because shepherds don't feed them. Shepherds don't feed them because shepherds don't have food." Martin leaned forward in his seat. "The shepherds don't have food *because they don't study their Bibles.*"

"You think it is obvious in the Word?"

"Certainly. When the apostle Paul magnified the pre-rogatives of the sovereign God, he fully anticipated the re-sponse of carnal reasoning." Martin leaned back, closed his eyes, and quoted, *"You will say to me then, 'why does He still find fault? For who has resisted His will?'* A modern pastor, in the unlikely event that someone asked him this, would say that it was a good question, and that he wrestles with it often himself. Paul tells the questioner to shut up and sit down. *But indeed, O man, who are you to reply against God?"*

"Paul doesn't answer the question then?"

Martin opened his eyes. "Oh, he does. It just isn't the answer carnal reason wants."

"So what is the answer?"

"The answer is God—the same answer that is given at the end of the book of Job. Carnal reason doesn't see a real answer there either. But believe me, it is a *real* answer. The answer is the ground of reality; the answer is *God."*

"What happens at the end of the book of Job?"

"The *questions* raised in the book are conducive to carnal reason; indeed, even non-Christians are attracted to the first part of the book of Job. As they would put it, 'It addresses the human condition.' But then, at the end of the book, *God* comes in, with glory and thunder. And do you know what? He doesn't answer any of the impertinent questions; rather, He poses some sobering questions of His own. *Who is this who darkens counsel by words without knowledge? Now prepare yourself like a man; I will question you, and you shall answer Me."*

I nodded. "And He asks where Job was when the universe was created."

"The question is not irrelevant. It is the heart of the matter. Discussions of God's sovereignty and human responsibility very rarely display any understanding at all of Who the *Creator* is."

"But my friends would say that you are making God responsible for evil, and that *they* are concerned to protect God's honor and glory."

Martin looked at me intently. "It is true that the affirmation of God's total control over all things causes some to blaspheme. But your friends need not be concerned for God's glory; man's slanders and blasphemies do not touch Him. Such slanderers are pelting the sun with wadded-up balls of tissue paper."

"They are stumbling over *something* though."

"They stumble, being disobedient to the Word, to which they also were appointed."

"Now, see? Why do you have to put these things so *strongly*? Doesn't that cause people to react to what you are teaching? They were *appointed* to stumble?"

"That wasn't my choice of words. I was quoting 1 Peter 2:8."

"Oh. Oops."

"Your friends are concerned that God be seen as *good*. But seen as good by whom? Those who believe the Word of God will know that God is light and in Him is no darkness at all. Of course He is good—*by definition*. And those who do not believe the Word of God will persist in thinking that there is a tribunal or court somewhere in which God will one day be arraigned. On the day of judgment, their folly will be apparent to all—even to them."

"So how do we bring this back to the original point?"

"The original point was the concern that the doctrine of God's sovereignty would be made into a cushion for sin. My answer to this is that we must, in all things, recognize God *as* God. We must do so in how we live holy lives, but we must also do so in *why* we live holy lives. We are to live in a holy way because God has commanded it."

"But would you also say that what God has *commanded* the believer He has also *given* the believer?"

"Well, certainly."

"I honestly see why carnal reason has a problem with this."

"And I honestly see why carnal men want to lust after beautiful women. But what does the Bible say?"

"What do you mean?"

"What is the greatest *commandment*?"

"That we love God."

"And what is the first *fruit* of the Spirit?"

"Love," I said. "I see."

"What do you see?" Martin asked.

"This takes us back to Philippians. We are commanded to work out what God works in."

"Right," he said. "Nothing less."

_____ five _____

Is God the Author of Sin?

"Surely," I said, "you don't believe God is the Author of sin?"

"You are right," he said. "I do not."

I sat back in my chair with some relief, although there was still an aspect of this that puzzled me.

Martin took up the slack in the conversation. "You perhaps are wondering how God can control sin completely without being the Author of it."

"That's right," I said.

"Let's begin where there is no disagreement. We all agree that God is not the Author of sin because Deuteronomy 32:4 says so. _He is the Rock, His work is perfect; for all His ways are justice, a God of truth and without injustice; righteous and upright is He._ And in James we are told that God tempts no one, and He Himself is not tempted."

"Fine."

"Now can this perfect God wield the imperfections of sinners to His own glory? Can He do this without being contaminated by the sin?"

"Well, I don't know. That's the question, isn't it?"

"It is a question carnal reason likes to ask. But it is not a question when it comes to the plain meaning of the text."

"Okay, okay. Where?"

"Let's start with the passage that speaks about the greatest wickedness ever done—the crucifixion of Christ."

"Which is. . . ?" I waited.

"Acts 4:27-28."

I turned to it and read. *For truly against Your holy Servant Jesus, whom You anointed, both Herod and Pontius Pilate, with the Gentiles and the people of Israel, were gathered together to do whatever Your hand and Your purpose determined before to be done.*

Martin asked, "What does it say?"

"It says that God planned the crucifixion."

"And was the crucifixion the work of evil men?"

"Yes. Doesn't Jesus tell Pilate that the *sin* of the Jews was greater than his? That implies that both were in sin."

"Right. And Peter, a couple of chapters before this one, charges his audience with this sin, even while he affirms God's control of it."

"Where is that?"

"Acts 2:23. *Him, being delivered by the determined counsel and foreknowledge of God, you have taken by lawless hands, have crucified, and put to death. . . .* This death of Christ was determined by God, and it was accomplished by *lawless* hands."

"It seems clear that God does use evil to accomplish His purpose."

"It is indisputable. In His governing of the world, God causes all things to come to pass, including the wickedness of creatures. He does this without in any way defiling Himself. Take the sin of Absalom, when he slept with his father's concubines, in the sight of all Israel. Was that a noble deed?"

"Certainly not."

"And what did God say through the prophet, before it had happened? 2 Samuel 12:11."

I turned rapidly to the place. *Thus says the Lord: "Behold I will raise up adversity against you from your own house; and I will take your wives before your eyes and give them to your neighbor, and he shall lie with your wives in the sight of this sun."*

"According to this, who gave the women to Absalom?"

"God did."

"And yet was it a wicked thing Absalom did? God gave

him the women, but he nevertheless had no right to them?"

"Yes."

"Now, do you believe this because you can reconcile it in your mind, or do you believe it because it is plainly taught in the Bible?"

"I know what you are asking. Those are two separate approaches to truth. I believe the second one is right, and I think I am getting there. But, honestly, I am not there yet."

"Let's look at one more section, okay?"

"Okay."

"Isaiah 10."

I turned there, and we both read through the chapter silently.

Martin broke the silence.

"God sent Assyria against the Jews as a military judgment, correct?"

"Right. It says, *I will send him against an ungodly nation. . . .*"

"And then does it say that Assyria will be judged for its pride? Verse 12?"

I nodded. "Yes."

"So God sent Assyria, and then judged Assyria for going?"

"Yes. Would it be right to say that God controlled Assyria's actions totally, and yet the arrogance and pride was not God's, but Assyria's?"

"That is exactly right. The pride of Assyria was seen in the denial that God was controlling them. And that is what the prophet addressed. *Shall the ax boast itself against him who chops with it? Or shall the saw magnify itself against him who saws with it?*"

I nodded again.

"I know this is hard for many Christians to accept. But this doctrine is the foundation of a precious truth in the Word."

"And what is that?"

"*All things work together for good—*"

"—*to those who love God, to those who are the called according to His purpose.* I get it!"

"What do you get?"

"In a world full of sin, God could not make such a promise to His people unless He had *complete* control over all evil. If He didn't, then that autonomous evil could harm a Christian, apart from God's plan."

We both sat in silence for a moment. "This is wonderful," I said.

Martin nodded. "It is wonderful."

_____ six _____

Controlled Freedom

"So you believe that God controls everything, right down to the last detail?"

"Yes. To the falling of sparrows. To the number of hairs on our heads. Nothing happens apart from the Father."

"God causes everything directly?"

"No, of course not. That would be a form of pantheism. If God does everything directly, there is no such thing as secondary agents—individuals other than God. I said that God _controls_ everything. Nothing, including the smallest detail, is outside His control."

"Does the Bible teach this?"

"Yes. Inescapably."

I took my Bible out. "All right. Where?"

"Is it safe to say you already believe that God providentially governs things like the physical world, and the animal kingdom? As in Amos 4:7, where the Lord causes rain to fall on one city, and not on another? Or in Matthew 6, where it teaches that the Father feeds the birds?"

"Right. There is no problem there. I am primarily concerned about His providential control over the free actions of men. Can God see to it that someone does just what God wants him to, and at the same time not violate the integrity of that person's free will?"

"Certainly. This is one of those subjects that has too many verses to go over in one session. I'll have to give you another list to study later. But there are a few passages worth addressing now."

"Shoot."

"Proverbs 21:1. *The king's heart is in the hand of the Lord, like the rivers of water; He turns it wherever He wishes.*"

"Boy," I said, "if anyone has free will a king should."

"A king does," Martin said. "Don't fall into the trap of thinking that these are truths which exclude one another. The Bible teaches that the king's heart is in the hand of the Lord. It also teaches us that kings, like all men, are responsible for what they do. A good example of God doing this to a king is found in Ezra 6:22."

"Are there other passages like this?"

"Sure. This is not a control that is limited to kings. Turn to Proverbs 16:9. *A man's heart plans his way, but the Lord directs his steps.*"

"Look at that," I said.

"Notice how the Lord controls what happens without violating the will of the creature. If a man plans to sin, God is not the *author* of it. Nevertheless, He *is* the perfect controller of it. The Lord directs the man's steps."

"I like that. Perfect control."

"When Judas went to betray the Lord, and when Pilate capitulated to the crowds, the Father was not wringing His hands in hopeless dismay. Angels were not running around heaven yelling, 'Plan B!'"

I laughed. "But those men were certainly sinning."

"Yes, they were. It was the most heinous crime our race has ever commited. And yet it was under God's perfect control."

"Right. We talked about that last week." I turned back to Acts 4:27-28 and read aloud. *For truly against Your holy Servant Jesus, whom You anointed, both Herod and Pontius Pilate, with the Gentiles and the people of Israel, were gathered together to do whatever Your hand and Your purpose determined before to be done.* I looked up.

Martin leaned forward. "It was the will of God that Jesus

die the way He did—for the salvation of sinners. But it was also the will of Pilate, and the will of the Jews, who were all fully blameworthy for what they did. Nevertheless, it was the hand and purpose of God that *determined beforehand* what was to be done."

"So it seems clear. God providentially controls everything. And He does so without violating the responsibility of His creatures."

"Yes. And, for theists, the only consistent alternative to this is some form of deism. God is considered by deists as the Creator of the universe, but now He is merely a spectator, if that."

"But the Bible teaches that God is *near*. . . . He is involved in everything that happens."

"Yes, that's right. And some Christians affirm this consistently, and others affirm it inconsistently. But all who acknowledge the Bible affirm it."

Texts on Providence

Proverbs 16:33
The lot is cast into the lap, but *its every decision* is from the Lord.

Proverbs 16:1
The preparations of the heart belong to man, but the answer of the tongue is *from the Lord.*

Isaiah 46:9-10
Remember the former things of old, for I am God, and there is no other; I am God, and there is none like Me, *declaring the end from the beginning*, and from ancient times things that are not yet done, saying 'My counsel shall stand, and *I will do all my pleasure. . . .*'

Psalm 139:16
Your eyes saw my substance, being yet unformed. And in Your book they all were written, *the days fashioned for me*, when as yet there were none of them.

1 Kings 22:28,34
Then Micaiah said, 'If you ever return in peace, the Lord has not spoken by me.' And he said, 'Take heed, all you people!'. . . Now a certain man drew a bow *at random*, and struck the king of Israel between the joints of his armor.

Mark 14:30
And Jesus said to him, 'Assuredly, I say to you that to-day, even this night, before the rooster crows twice, *you will deny Me* three times.'

Luke 22:22
And truly the Son of Man goes as it has been *determined*, but woe to that man by whom He is betrayed!

Job 14:5

Since his days are *determined*, the number of his months is with You; You have appointed his limits, so that he cannot pass.

Genesis 50:20

But as for you, you meant evil against me; *but God meant it for good*, in order to bring it about as it is this day, to save many people alive.

Isaiah 45:7

I form the light and create darkness, I make peace and create calamity; *I, the Lord, do all these things.*

Amos 3:6

If a trumpet is blown in a city, will not the people be afraid? If there is calamity in a city, *will not the Lord have done it?*

seven

Potters and Pots

"What do you mean, it's like a play?" I asked.

"I mean that God is the Author, and we are the characters."

"I know I have some objections already. But explain some more first."

"All right. We persist, in discussions of this issue, in talking as though God were a fellow-character in the play. But He is not. Our relationship to him is not that of Macbeth to Duncan, but rather of Macbeth to Shakespeare."

"What does this help explain?"

"If an English teacher asked her students why Macbeth did thus and such, one answer could be that he wanted to be king, and so forth. The student could answer in terms of Macbeth's motivations and so on."

"Is another answer possible?"

"Sure. Macbeth did what he did because that is the way Shakespeare wrote the play. Now both answers are true—but they apply at different levels."

"But that doesn't make sense to me. Macbeth is a *fictional* character. It doesn't matter if he has free will or not. Surely our decisions and lives are much greater than his, are they not?"

"Certainly. And God is much greater than Shakespeare."

I slumped back in my chair. "Don't you think your analogy breaks down at all?"

"Well, of course . . . at some point. Whenever I use the analogy of a play, people object and say that we are greater than mere fictional characters. But the same objection can be leveled against the biblical analogy of the Potter and His pots. We are more than mere pots. And Paul agrees with this, even while he is using the analogy. *But indeed, O man, who are you to reply against God? Will the thing formed say to him who formed it, 'Why have you made me like this?'* Paul declares that we are fashioned according to the will of the Potter, and in the same breath, he blames those pots who think otherwise. He clearly assigns personal responsibility to pots. And the analogy remains a good one."

"So where does the analogy break down?"

"In two places. The first place is the obvious one—the one everyone seizes upon. We are more than pots, or fictional characters in a play."

"Where is the second place?"

"I mentioned it before. God is much greater than a potter, or an author of a play."

"Could you please expound?"

"When we compare pots and potters, or authors and plays, we are comparing something finite with something finite. So, although the gap between a potter and his pots is great, it is not infinite."

"But. . . ?"

"But when we compare the Creator with His creation, there is an infinite gulf between the two."

I could feel a headache starting.

"So how would this apply?"

"Our great objection, proud pots that we are, is the great distance between us and earthenware pots. There must be ten feet, at least. Not concerned for the glory of God, we don't even notice the infinite number of light years between God and potters."

I felt myself starting to catch a glimmer of what Martin was saying. "I think I get it. You are saying that the distance between us and God is greater than the distance between potters and pots."

"Right. The analogy does break down, but not in a way that soothes the injured pride of pots."

"So what would you say to those who objected to your analogy?"

"I would have two responses. One, I would ask them to show me how my example of the play differs in any essential detail from the biblical analogy of potters and pots. If they cannot, then every objection they bring would bear equally on inspired Scripture."

"And what would be your second response?"

"I would ask this: if the finite Shakespeare can produce, by his will, fictional characters who have all the freedom necessary for their 'level of existence,' then why cannot the infinite God create real individuals, with real free agency, without surrendering His control?"

"You are saying that because God's resources are infinitely greater than Shakespeare's, He has the power to write history and create characters who have true freedom."

"Yes . . . without having His characters write the play."

"I don't get it."

Martin laughed, and leaned forward. "Neither do I."

"Now I don't get *that*. If you don't get it, why do you believe it?"

"Because I was told to. This is not truth presented to me by some explorer, or scientist. It was revealed in the Bible. If it had not been, I would not have to believe it. God does not demand that I *understand* Him, or understand all His relations to His creation. And I don't understand Him."

"But you do believe Him. . . ?"

Martin smiled. "I do believe Him."

_____ eight _____

Election

"What about election?" I asked.

Martin laughed. "What about it?"

"Well, the Bible clearly teaches that there is a group of people called the elect. It seems to me that the heart of the debate between Christians is over why they are called that, and how they came to be elect."

"That is exactly right. That is the issue."

"Mind if I try a few thoughts out on you?"

"Be my guest."

"Do we agree that God knows everything, including the future?"

Martin nodded. "Certainly. But you do realize that some professing Christians, for the sake of evading God's exhaustive sovereignty, have denied even that."

My eyes widened. "No, I didn't know that." I paused for a moment. "But _we_ surely agree that He knows beforehand who will believe in Him, and who will not?"

"That is correct."

"Couldn't we say then, that God made His choice of certain individuals based on His foreknowledge of faith? That way, God chooses, and men have no one to blame but themselves if they are not chosen."

Martin thought for a moment.

"And what would the scriptural evidence for this theory be?"

53

"Well, 1 Peter 1:2 says that certain Christians were elect according to the *foreknowledge* of God the Father. And Romans 8:28 says something very similar. It says that those whom God *foreknew*, He predestined. . . ."

"Very well. Let's return to the whole idea of foreknowledge in a moment. But before we do that, we should carefully set out what you are saying."

"Fair enough."

"At some time in eternity, God looked down the corridors of time, into the future, and saw that Jones would have faith in Him, and that Smith would not."

"Right."

"On that basis, God elected Jones to salvation, and did not elect Smith."

"Right again."

"Now in this scenario, is God doing anything more than echoing the choice of Jones?"

"What do you mean?"

"It sounds like Jones is saying that he wants to be saved, and as a consequence, God says, 'Me, too!' Is that all election is?"

"I wouldn't put it that way. God still makes the choice."

"Yes, but God makes His choice based upon the choice of the man. This is the basic difference: one position says that God's choices are based on man's choices, while the other position says that man's choices are based on God's."

"I see. Both sides agree that man chooses, and both agree that God chooses. They differ over which is the foundational choice."

"Correct. And in making man's choice foundational, the biblical terminology is stood on its head."

"What do you mean?"

"Instead of *many are called, but few are chosen*, it becomes *many are called but few choose*. Instead of God's elect, we become God's electors."

"I agree that you have a point in many passages. But how would you handle the verses I used earlier?"

"Let's start with Peter. Notice what he does not say. He says nothing about cognitive foreknowledge of *choices*. He merely says that God's elect were elect according to the fore-knowledge of the Father. The text does not tell us the content of that foreknowledge. Because both positions agree that God's election is according to foreknowledge, this verse proves nothing either way."

"What about Romans 8?"

"That passage *does* tell us the object of God's foreknowl-edge. The object of His foreknowledge is not history, or choices, seen apart from His sovereign government. The object of His foreknowledge here is persons. Those *whom* He foreknew, He predestined."

"I agree that is what is says. But what does foreknowl-edge mean then?"

"The Greek word here in Romans is *proginosko*. The prefix *pro* means *before*, while the word *ginosko* has two meanings; one means *to know*, while the other means *to approve*. One of the meanings of this compound verb is *to approve beforehand*. Now if you put that understanding into the Romans 8 pas-sage, how does it read?"

"For whom he approved beforehand, He also predestined to be conformed. . ." I broke off. "I see! Predestination here is not to 'becoming a Christian,' but to 'becoming Christ-like' at the resurrection."

Martin smiled. "Exactly. Those on whom God set His electing love, He predestined to a final conformity to the image of Christ. And Paul follows this wonderful chain of redemption right to the end in verse 30."

I looked at the passage again. *Moreover whom He pre-destined, these He also called; whom He called, these He also justified; and whom He justified, these He also glorified.*

I looked up from the page. "But wait a minute. Couldn't someone object that our choice of 'approve beforehand' is a case of special pleading? Why couldn't it be translated the other way?"

Martin leaned forward in his chair. "Because the other

way doesn't make any sense, for *either* position."

"What?"

"In our discussions, I think you will see this again and again. Many of the verses brought to bear against this understanding of God's sovereignty have this in common. They invariably *prove too much.*"

"What do you mean, prove too much?"

"If foreknowledge is simply referring to cognitive information, then this is the chain of redemption. 'For whom He foreknew (everyone), He also predestined to Christ-likeness (everyone). Whom He predestined, He called (everyone), and whom He called, He justified (everyone). Whom He justified, He glorified (everyone).' There is no place for any individuals to escape. Everyone cognitively foreknown will be glorified. And that is universalism."

"Hold on, hold on! I didn't say that God foreknew *everyone*. I said that He foreknew those who would believe in Him."

"But the passage doesn't say *that*. That is something which has to be imported into the text. The object of His foreknowledge is persons, not actions, and there is no ground in the text for making it *believing persons*. That *would* be special pleading."

I sat thinking for a moment. Martin continued.

"There is another reason for denying that God elects based upon His foresight of our doings."

"What is that?"

"Express statements to the contrary in Scripture."

"All right, I'm game. Show me one."

"Turn to 2 Timothy 1:8-9."

I turned and read. *Therefore do not be ashamed of the testimony of our Lord, nor of me His prisoner, but share with me in the sufferings for the gospel according to the power of God, who has saved us and called us with a holy calling, not according to our works, but according to His own purpose and grace which was given to us in Christ Jesus before time began.*

"Allow me to ask you a few questions."

"Go ahead," I replied.

"What has God done for us?"

"He saved us and called us."

"Correct. And He did this *not* according to something. . . ."

"Not according to our works."

"Correct again. Now, our works are set in contrast to that by which He *did* save and call us. What was that?"

"His own purpose and grace."

"Does the passage contrast *our* works with *our* faith?"

"No. It contrasts our works with His purpose and grace."

"Very good. Now where was this given to us?"

"*Where?*"

"Uh-huh."

"In Christ? Is that what you mean?"

"Right. *When* was it given?"

"Before time began."

"So God saved and called us with a holy calling, before the beginning of time, and He did this without reference to our works."

"Well, that is true. But how can you classify foreseen faith as a form of foreseen works? Faith is not a work."

"*True* faith is not a work because true faith is a gift from God. But if faith is something man does, on his own, and which appropriates salvation, which another man does not receive because he did not believe, then faith is a work."

"I'm sorry, I don't see what you are driving at. How can faith be a work?"

"One of the reasons people object to the idea of faith as a gift from God is that they think such gifts remove the possibility of praise or blame. It turns man into a puppet—that sort of thing. Isn't that right?"

"Well, yes."

"Now how can they insist that we keep faith as something man does—otherwise we cannot praise or blame him for having or not having it—but then object when someone says they have made faith a work? True praise or blame, according to this kind of thinking, can only be assigned to a man's work."

"I've got it. You are saying that if it merits praise or blame then it is a work. If it doesn't merit praise or blame, then the objection against faith being a gift is gone."

"That's it. So then, God elects, according to His own good purpose (and it *is* good, not arbitrary), and He does so without regard to foreseen human achievement, virtue, works, or *meritorious* faith."

"I've heard this doctrine called unconditional election. Is that what the unconditional refers to?"

"Yes. It does not mean that God had no conditions or reasons for doing what He did. It simply means He found no conditions or reasons *in man* for what He did."

I sat back in my chair. "It looks to me as though you have a point." We both laughed, and I got up to go.

Texts on the Election of the Father

Matthew 11:27

All things have been delivered to Me by My Father, and no one knows the Son except the Father. Nor does anyone know the Father except the Son, *and he to whom the Son wills to reveal Him.*

1 Peter 2:8-9

They stumble, being disobedient to the word, *to which they also were appointed.* But you are a *chosen* generation, a royal priesthood, a holy nation, *His own special people,* that you may proclaim the praises of Him who *called* you out of darkness into His marvelous light. . . .

2 Timothy 1:8-9

Therefore do not be ashamed of the testimony of our Lord, nor of me His prisoner, but share with me in the sufferings for the gospel according to the power of God, who has saved us and called us with a holy calling, *not according to our works, but according to His own purpose and grace which was given to us in Christ Jesus before time began. . .*

Deuteronomy 10:14-15

Indeed heaven and the highest heavens belong to the Lord your God, also the earth with all that is in it. The Lord *delighted only* in your fathers, *to love them*; and *He chose* their descendants after them, you above all peoples, as it is this day.

Psalm 33:12

Blessed is the nation whose God is the Lord, and the people *whom He has chosen* as His own inheritance.

Luke 18:7

And shall God not avenge *His own elect* who cry out day and night to Him, though He bears long with them?

Matthew 24:24
For false christs and false prophets will arise and show great signs and wonders, so as to deceive, if possible, *even the elect*.

Matthew 22:14
For many are called, but *few are chosen*.

Matthew 24:31
And He will send His angels with a great sound of a trumpet, and they will gather together *His elect* from the four winds, from one end of heaven to the other.

Luke 10:21-22
In that hour Jesus rejoiced in the Spirit and said, 'I praise You, Father, Lord of heaven and earth, that *You have hidden these things* from the wise and prudent and revealed them to babes. Even so, Father, for *so it seemed good in Your sight*. All things have been delivered to Me by My Father, and no one knows who the Son is but the Father, and who the Father is but the Son, *and the one to whom the Son wills to reveal Him*.'

Romans 8:28
And we know that all things work together for good to those who love God, *to those who are the called according to His purpose*.

Romans 8:33
Who shall bring a charge against *God's elect*? It is God who justifies.

1 Thessalonians 5:9
For God did not appoint *us* to wrath, *but to obtain salvation* through our Lord Jesus Christ.

Colossians 3:12
Therefore, *as the elect of God*, holy and beloved, put on

tender mercies, kindness, humbleness of mind, meekness, longsuffering. . . .

Titus 1:1
Paul, a servant of God and an apostle of Jesus Christ, according to the faith of *God's elect* and the acknowledgment of the truth which is according to godliness. . . .

1 Peter 1:1-2
Peter, an apostle of Jesus Christ, to the pilgrims of the Dispersion in Pontus, Galatia, Cappadocia, Asia, and Bithynia, *elect according to the foreknowledge of God the Father*, in sanctification of the Spirit, for obedience and sprinkling of the blood of Jesus Christ: Grace to you and peace be multiplied.

Revelation 17:14
These will make war with the Lamb, and the Lamb will overcome them, for He is Lord of lords and King of kings; and those who are with Him are *called, chosen, and faithful*.

Mark 13:20
And unless the Lord had shortened those days, no flesh would be saved; but for *the elect's* sake, *whom He chose*, He shortened the days.

Ephesians 1:4
Just as *He chose us* in Him before the foundation of the world, that we should be holy and without blame before Him in love. . . .

2 Thessalonians 2:13-14
But we are bound to give thanks to God always for you, brethren beloved by the Lord, because *God from the beginning chose you for salvation* through sanctification by the Spirit and belief in the truth, to which He called you by our gospel, for the obtaining of the glory of our Lord Jesus Christ.

Revelation 17:8

And those who dwell on the earth will marvel, *whose names are not written in the Book of Life from the foundation of the world*, when they see the beast that was, and is not, and yet is.

Romans 9:10-24

Not only this, but when Rebecca also had conceived by one man, even by our father Isaac (for the children not yet being born, *nor having done any good or evil, that the purpose of God according to election might stand, not of works but of Him who calls*), it was said to her, 'The older shall serve the younger.' And it is written, *'Jacob I have loved, but Esau I have hated.'*

What shall we say then? Is there unrighteousness with God? Certainly not! For He says to Moses, *'I will have mercy on whomever I will have mercy, and I will have compassion on whomever I will have compassion.'*

So then it is *not* of him who *wills,* nor of him who *runs,* but of *God* who shows mercy.

For the Scripture says to Pharaoh, 'Even for this same purpose I have raised you up, that I might show My power in you, and that My name might be declared in all the earth.'

Therefore *He has mercy on whom He wills,* and *whom He wills He hardens.* You will say to me then, 'Why does He still find fault? For who has resisted His will?'

But indeed, O man, who are you to reply against God? Will the thing formed say to him who formed it, 'Why have you made me like this?' Does not the potter have power over the clay, for the same lump to make one vessel for honor and another for dishonor? What if God, wanting to show His wrath and to make His power known, endured with much longsuffering the *vessels of wrath prepared for destruction,* and that He might make known the riches of His glory on the vessels of mercy, *which He had prepared beforehand for glory, even us whom He called,* not of the Jews only, but also of the Gentiles?

Romans 10:20
But Isaiah is very bold and says:
'I was found by those who did not seek Me;
I was made manifest to those who did not ask for Me.'

1 Corinthians 1:27-29
But *God has chosen* the foolish things of the world to put
to shame the wise, and *God has chosen* the weak things of
the world to put to shame the things which are mighty; and
the base things of the world and the things which are despised *God has chosen*, and the things that are not, to bring
to nothing the things that are, that no flesh should glory in
His presence.

Ephesians 1:11-12
In whom also we have obtained an inheritance, being
*predestined according to the purpose of Him who works all things
according to the counsel of His will*, that we who first trusted in
Christ should be to the praise of His glory.

Ephesians 2:10
For we are His workmanship, created in Christ Jesus for
good works, which *God prepared beforehand* that we should
walk in them.

John 15:16
You did not choose Me, but I chose you and appointed you
that you should go and bear fruit, and that your fruit should
remain, that whatever you ask the Father in My name He
may give you.

Philippians 2:12-13
Therefore, my beloved, as you have always obeyed, not
as in my presence only, but now much more in my absence,
work out your own salvation with fear and trembling; *for it is
God who works in you both to will and to do for His good pleasure.*

Acts 18:27

And when he desired to cross to Achaia, the brethren wrote, exhorting the disciples to receive him; and when he arrived, he greatly helped those *who had believed through grace.* . . .

Acts 13:48

Now when the Gentiles heard this, they were glad and glorified the word of the Lord. *And as many as had been appointed to eternal life believed.*

Philippians 1:29

For to you it has been *granted* on behalf of Christ, *not only to believe in Him,* but also to suffer for His sake. . . .

1 Thessalonians 1:4-5

Knowing, beloved brethren, *your election by God.* For our gospel did not come to you in word only, but also in power, and in the Holy Spirit and in much assurance, as you know what kind of men we were among you for your sake.

James 2:5

Listen, my beloved brethren: *Has God not chosen* the poor of this world to be rich in faith and heirs of the kingdom which He promised to those who love Him?

Romans 11:5-8

Even so then, at this present time there is a remnant according to *the election of grace.* And if by grace, then it is not longer works; otherwise grace is no longer grace. But if it is of works, it is no longer grace; otherwise work is no longer work. What then? Israel has not obtained what it seeks; but *the elect have obtained it,* and *the rest were hardened.* Just as it is written:

'*God has given them* a spirit of stupor,
Eyes that they should not see
And ears that they should not hear, to this very day.'

_____ nine _____

Gifts and Wages

On this particular evening, I began with a question one of my friends had asked me the previous week. I had not been able to answer her, but told her that I would try to check on it.

"So, are you teaching that God created certain people simply in order to damn them? And how could that be just?"

Martin smiled as though this were not the first time he had been asked this.

"No, I am not saying that."

"But isn't that what the doctrine of election logically entails?"

"No, not at all. Carnal reason would extend this from the doctrine of election, but that is not the way it is presented in the Bible at all."

"How so?"

"The Bible does not say that the gift of God to one group is eternal life, while His gift to the other group is eternal death."

"How does the Bible put it, then?"

"It says the _gift_ of God is life, and that the _wages_ of sin is death. God's treatment of the elect and those He passes by is _not_ symmetrical."

Inside, I was scratching my head. "Could you put it another way?"

"Sure. Why are certain men condemned by God?"

"You tell me."

"The answer of the Bible is straightforward. Men are condemned for their sins. When God damns a man, He is paying him a wage. It is strict justice. But when God sends a man to Heaven, it is the result of mercy. When I say the two are not symmetrical, I mean God is not giving two different kinds of gifts, or paying two different kinds of wages. It is a gift to one, and a paycheck to the other."

"What are some of the ramifications of this?"

"Well, first, it means that the one receiving the paycheck cannot object to the gift the other receives on the grounds of justice. For what he is receiving *is* justice. Nor can others object on his behalf."

"Why does it *seem* so unfair then?"

"Because we are proud, and *grace* is humbling."

"No, wait. Suppose a man had three kids, and he pours out his favor on just one? Isn't he showing partiality? And doesn't the Bible say that God doesn't show partiality?"

"But the example you give is misleading, and does not adequately represent the case we are discussing. At conversion, we *become* children of God. It is not something we have automatically. For a more appropriate example, suppose a governor, for reasons of his own, signs a pardon for one death row inmate. Has he done an injustice to the others on death row? If they die, do they not deserve it?"

"But how can he be just in letting this guilty one go free?"

"Now *that* is a good question. We are now dealing with a biblical problem. How can God be just *and* the one who justifies? The answer given to this problem in the Bible is the cross. In the cross, mercy is shown to sinners, and justice is not compromised."

"Go on."

"The problem is *not* why God hated Esau. The problem concerns how He could love Jacob."

"All right. So could you return to your point about grace?"

"All Christians agree that grace is a gift, correct?"

"That's right."

"And you will hear many of them say that the gift is un-deserved."

"That's right, too."

"Now does God have the right to give this gift to some, and not to others? If He does this, is He unjust?"

"If it is an undeserved gift, then I suppose there can be no injustice in withholding it. . . from all, or some." I wasn't sure I liked what I was saying, or where this was heading.

"Now if someone hears me saying that the gift was with-held from someone, and he responds by saying that this is unjust, is he not saying that the gift must be given *as a matter of justice?*"

"Yes, he is saying that."

"So then God *owes* grace to this man?"

"Well, the conclusion seems inescapable."

"And if grace is owed, how is it grace? How can an un-deserved gift be something I have a right to demand?"

"It cannot be."

I thought for a moment, and then spoke again.

"Suppose someone granted your point, and said that God *could*, without injustice, pass certain people by. Couldn't they then go on, and argue that, nevertheless, He did not pass anyone by, even though He could have, but rather bestows grace on all?"

"Yes, they could say that, and frankly, it would be quite refreshing. I have grown tired of hearing Christians level the same charge against God that Paul refers to in Romans 9, that is, why does He still blame us, and so forth."

I grinned. "All right. Having been refreshed, how would you respond?"

"Once people have surrendered the charge of injustice, the question becomes simply a textual one. Does the Bible teach that God has passed anyone by with regard to salva-tion? The answer is yes."

"Okay, where?"

"Here are several worth considering. Turn to Romans 11:7-8."

I flipped through the pages, and read aloud. *"What then? Israel has not obtained what it seeks; but the elect have obtained it, and the rest were hardened. Just as it is written: 'God has given them a spirit of stupor, eyes that they should not see and ears that they should not hear, to this very day.'"* I looked up.

Martin looked at me carefully. "Apart from any system of doctrine, what do these words say? Did Israel obtain what it sought?"

"No."

"Who did obtain it?"

"The elect."

"What happened to those who were not elect?"

"They were hardened."

"This was according to what?"

"The Old Testament." I looked at the margin in my Bible. "Isaiah and Deuteronomy."

"These who were hardened. . . what was given to them?"

"A spirit of stupor."

"Who gave this spirit of stupor?"

"God."

"Did he give anything else?"

"Yes. Unseeing eyes, and unhearing ears."

"Why?"

"So that they would not hear or see."

"How long did this blind and deaf condition last?"

"Well, at least up to the writing of Romans."

Martin leaned back in his chair. "Now did I ask you anything about the theology of Calvin or Augustine?"

"No, not at all."

"Turn to John 12:37-40."

"All right."

I turned to the passage, and read aloud again. *"But although He had done so many signs before them, they did not believe in Him, that the word of Isaiah the prophet might be fulfilled, which he spoke: 'Lord, who has believed our report? And to whom has the arm of the Lord been revealed?' Therefore they could not believe, because Isaiah said again: 'He has blinded their eyes and hardened their heart, lest they should see with their eyes and understand with their heart, lest they should turn, so that I should heal them.'"*

Martin looked at me. "Let's pass on another series of questions. What does this passage *say*, quite apart from what we might think it means?"

"Well, it says that certain first century Jews did not believe in Jesus, in spite of the miracles, in order that Isaiah's prophecy might be fulfilled. It goes on to say they *could* not believe because of another prophecy in Isaiah. That prophecy says that God blinded their eyes, and hardened their hearts lest they should repent, and be healed."

"Very good. And are these the words of men?"

"No, I don't think they are." I said. "They are the words of God."

_____ ten _____

Definite Atonement

I stirred nervously in my seat, and cleared my throat. I was not at all sure I wanted to ask the next question, but I also realized I had to.

"You have already told me you have no desire to be called a 'Calvinist.'"

"That is correct," Martin nodded.

"Is this just a concern over party labels, or is there any key theological area where you disagree with the Calvinists?"

"How do you mean?"

"Well, I was talking with someone at my home church, and he told me something that horrified me. He said that Calvinists believe in something they call *limited atonement*. They think that Jesus only died for Christians, and not for all men."

Martin laughed, and then said, "I'll answer your question, if you promise to hear me out."

I had a sinking feeling that this meant he *did* believe it, but I nodded my head anyway.

"First, all orthodox Christians believe in a limited atonement. Every Christian who believes that there is an eternal Hell limits the atonement. One group limits its power or effectiveness, and the other limits its extent. But both limit the atonement."

I nodded, so he went on.

"Secondly, I don't know who came up with the phrase *limited atonement* to describe this position. He may have been a theological genius, but when it comes to public relations, he must have been a chucklehead."

"In what way?" I asked.

"One fellow says he believes in a *limited* atonement, and another says he believes in an *unlimited* atonement. Which one appears to be doing justice to the Scriptures?"

"The second one, of course."

Martin smiled. "Of course. God so loved the *world*; Behold the Lamb of God who takes away the sin of the *world*; One died for *all*, and so forth."

I nodded again, wondering where on earth he was going.

"Now suppose we hear the same two fellows, but this time the language is changed. The first says now that he believes in a *definite* atonement, and the second affirms his belief in an *indefinite* atonement. Who sounds more biblical now?"

"Well, now the first sounds more biblical."

"Of course. Christ laid down His life for the *sheep*; Christ loved the *church* and gave Himself for it; and He gave Himself up, that He might *redeem us* from every lawless deed. When He went to the cross, Christ had a definite end in view for a definite group of people."

"Okay. Then it seems to me that when it is put the first way it shows that one group does justice to the universality of the redemption, and when it is put the second way, it shows that their theological opponents do justice to the efficient purpose of the redemption. And both sides have their verses."

"But both sides, if they believe that the whole Bible is from God, must affirm both types of verses."

"How can you do that? If you believe in a definite atonement, how can you square that with some of the *universal* passages you quoted earlier?"

"One of the reasons I object so strongly to terms like *limited atonement* is that it does nothing but reinforce a theological caricature that many have in their minds. I believe that Jesus purchased a definite number of people when He died. But there is no reason we must believe that the number was a small one. He came into the world to save the world, and He will be content with nothing less than a *saved world*."

"Do you believe that there will be more people saved than lost?"

"Certainly. It says in 1 John 2:2 that He is the propitiation for our sins, and not for ours only but also for *the whole world*."

"Wait a minute," I said. "That just means that every person can be forgiven for their sins if they come to Christ."

"But that is not what it says. It says that Christ was the propitiation for the whole world. Propitiation means that God's wrath is turned aside. If Christ is the propitiation for the sins of the whole world, then God's wrath is turned away from the whole world."

I sat silently for a moment, and Martin went on.

"Notice how the verse does *not* read. It doesn't say that He is the propitiation for our sins, because we believed, and not only for ours, but He is a potential propitiation for the whole world, if only they believe, but of course we know they won't."

I laughed. "Well, I agree it doesn't say *that*."

"See, the difficulty with verses like this, from the universalist standpoint, is that they prove too much."

"What do you mean by that?"

"The Bible teaches that Christ's death is *powerful to save*. This power comes through in many of the universal passages. So I reject the position that wants the universality of the passage, but not the efficacy of it. In other words, there is no *potential* propitiation in 1 John 2:2. It is actual. *Real*. In the cross of Christ, the wrath of God has been turned aside *from the world*."

"Does this present any Calvinists with a problem?"

"It surely does. When the Bible speaks of *all men*, or the

world, there is no grammatical reason in Greek to refer it to each and every man. But at the same time, I believe it is impossible to refer such wonderful universal statements to a tiny snippet of humanity."

"I don't understand you."

"Suppose you went to a football game at your school, and the attendance was spectacular. Would you be lying if you said that the whole student body was there, when in fact Jones was in his room sick?"

I laughed. "No."

"But suppose you said the whole student body was there, when it was just you and Jones. Would there be a problem now?"

"Certainly."

"Because. . . ?"

"Because in the first instance my language would not be at all misleading, while in the second instance it would be."

"Correct. Those who believe what the Bible says about election, but who believe the elect to be few in number, have the same problem. They are confronted with glorious texts about a saved world, and they turn them into texts about a saved church, comprised of the few that will be saved. Of course, their theological opponents are not much better. They turn glorious texts about a saved world into texts about a world which *could* be saved, but probably won't be."

"So if we continue in this vein, we will no longer be talking about the atonement, but rather eschatology?"

"Well, yes. Although my eschatology is based on this understanding of the atonement, it would take us off track at the present. Some future discussion perhaps? It should suffice to say that the Bible teaches us about an atonement that is efficacious and definite on the one hand, and universal on the other. All those for whom Christ died will be saved, and Christ died for the world."

"And you are saying that this is different than saying Christ died for each and every person."

"Yes. The problem people have with this comes from assuming that both sides of this dispute mean the same thing by *for*."

"What do you mean?"

"Given that not all men are saved, contrast these two statements: First, Christ died for each and every man. Second, Christ died for His people.

"The word *for* has a completely different meaning in each of these sentences. In the first, it means that Christ died in order to provide an *opportunity* of salvation to each and every man. In the second, it means He died to *secure* the salvation of His people. So the debate is not about the *extent* of the atonement so much as it is about the *nature* of the atonement."

"Can you illustrate what you mean?"

"Sure. Suppose you have a philanthropist giving away money. He walks down the street handing out $100 bills. It is easy to assume (falsely) that the one position says he gives $100 to everybody, while the other side maintains he will give money to only some of the people. In this scenario, the debate is about the *extent* of generosity, and whether or not the philanthropist is being stingy. But on this understanding, both sides agree that the *gift* is the same (money), while the generosity varies."

"Okay," I said. "What *is* the debate about?"

"In one view, the philanthropist is not giving out $100 bills. He is giving out tickets to an awards ceremony, where every person attending will be given $100, *if* they decide to show up. He is giving away an *opportunity* to get $100. This contrasts with the other view which has the philanthropist out in the street, stuffing the money into pockets. He is not giving away opportunity; he is giving away money. So now the debate is over the *nature* of the gift. Is the gift money, or an opportunity to receive money?"

I thought for a moment. "So in the area of salvation, you are saying that Christ did not die to give men the opportunity of redemption, if they believe, but that He died to redeem men."

"You've got it."

"Well, I think I understand it anyway. But you'll have to excuse me if I don't accept what you are saying right off. This is going to take some hard thinking and Bible study."

"That is exactly what it takes. And don't rush it. Don't agree to anything until you see it in the Scriptures. So which does the Bible teach? Redemption, or an opportunity to be redeemed?"

Texts on the Atonement

2 Corinthians 5:21

For He made Him who knew no sin to be sin for us, *that we might become* the righteousness of God in Him.

Galatians 1:3-5

Grace to you and peace from God the Father and our Lord Jesus Christ, who gave Himself for our sins, *that He might deliver us* from this present evil age, *according to the will of our God and Father*, to whom be glory forever and ever. Amen.

Titus 2:14

Who gave Himself for us, *that He might redeem us* from every lawless deed and purify for Himself *His own special people*, zealous for good works.

1 Peter 3:18

For Christ also suffered once for sins, the just for the unjust, *that He might bring us to God*, being put to death in the flesh but made alive by the Spirit.

Ephesians 5:25-27

Husbands, love your wives, just as Christ also loved the church and *gave Himself for it*, *that* He might sanctify and cleanse it with the washing of water by the word, *that* He might present it to Himself a glorious church, not having spot or wrinkle or any such thing, but *that* it should be holy and without blemish.

Hebrews 13:12

Therefore, Jesus also, *that He might sanctify the people with His own blood*, suffered outside the gate.

Matthew 20:28

Just as the Son of Man did not come to be served, but to serve, and to give His life a ransom for *many*.

John 10:10

The thief does not come except to steal, and to kill, and to destroy. *I have come that they may have life*, and that they may have it more abundantly.

John 10:14-18

I am the good shepherd; and *I know My sheep*, and am known by My own. As the Father knows Me, even so I know the Father; *and I lay down My life for the sheep*. And other sheep I have which are not of this fold; them also I must bring, and they will hear My voice; and there will be one flock and one shepherd. Therefore My Father loves Me, because I lay down My life that I may take it again. No one takes it from Me, but I lay it down of Myself. I have power to lay it down, and I have power to take it again. This command I have received from My Father.

John 10:25-30

Jesus answered them, 'I told you, and you do not believe. The works that I do in My Father's name, they bear witness of Me. But you do not believe, *because you are not of My sheep*, as I said to you. *My sheep* hear My voice, and I know them, and they follow Me. *And I give them eternal life*, and they shall never perish; neither shall anyone snatch them out of My hand. My Father, who has given them to Me, is greater than all; and no one is able to snatch them out of My Father's hand. I and My Father are one.'

John 17:1-11

Jesus spoke these words, lifted up His eyes to heaven, and said: 'Father, the hour has come. Glorify Your Son, that Your Son also may glorify You, as You have given Him authority over all flesh, *that He should give eternal life to as many as You have given Him*. And this is eternal life, that they may know You, the only true God, and Jesus Christ whom You have sent. I have glorified You on the earth. I have finished the work which You have given Me to do.

And now, O Father, glorify Me together with Yourself, with the glory which I had with You before the world was.

I have manifested Your name to the men *whom You have given Me out of the world.* They were Yours, You gave them to Me, and they have kept Your word.

Now they have known that all things which You have given Me are from You. For I have given to them the words which You have given Me; and they have received them, and have known surely that I came forth from You; and they have believed that You sent Me.

I pray for them. *I do not pray for the world but for those whom You have given Me,* for they are Yours.

And all Mine are Yours, and Yours are Mine, and I am glorified in them.

Now I am no longer in the world, but these are in the world, and I come to You. Holy Father, keep through Your name those *whom You have given Me,* that they may be one as We are.'

John 17:20

I do not pray for these alone, but *also* for those who will believe in Me through their word. . . .

John 17:24-26

Father, I desire that they also whom You gave Me may be with Me where I am, that they may behold My glory which You have given Me; for You loved Me before the foundation of the world.

O righteous Father! The world has not known You, but I have known You; and these have known that You sent Me. And I have declared to them Your name, and will declare it, that the love with which You loved Me may be in them, and I in them.

Matthew 26:28

For this is My blood of the new covenant, which is shed for *many* for the remission of sins.

Romans 5:12

Therefore, *just as* through one man sin entered the world, and death through sin, and thus death spread to all men, because all sinned. . . .

Romans 5:17-19

(For if by the one man's offense death reigned through the one, *much more those who receive abundance of grace and of the gift of righteousness* will reign in life through the One, Jesus Christ.)

For as by one man's disobedience many were made sinners, *so also by one Man's obedience many will be made righteous*.

John 11:49-52

And one of them, Caiaphas, being high priest that year, said to them, 'You know nothing at all, nor do you consider that it is expedient for us that one man should die for the people, and not that the whole nation should perish.'

Now this he did not say on his own authority; but being high priest that year he prophesied that Jesus would die for the nation, *and not for that nation only, but also that He would gather together in one the children of God who were scattered abroad*.

Romans 8:32-33

He who did not spare His own Son, *but delivered Him up for us all*, how shall He not with Him also freely give *us* all things? Who shall bring a charge against *God's elect?* It is God who justifies.

Hebrews 9:15

And for this reason He is the Mediator of the new covenant, *by means of death*, for the redemption of the transgressions under the first covenant, *that those who are called may receive* the promise of the eternal inheritance.

Hebrews 9:27-28

And as it is appointed for men to die once, but after this the judgment, so Christ was offered once to bear the sins of *many*. To those who eagerly wait for Him He will appear a second time, apart from sin, for salvation.

Revelation 5:9

And they sang a new song, saying:
'You are worthy to take the scroll,
And to open its seals;
For You were slain,
And *have redeemed us to God by your blood*
Out of every tribe and tongue and people and nation,
And have made us kings and priests to our God;
And we shall reign on the earth.'

_____ eleven _____

Regeneration

I had thought of a question during the week which I thought would bring our conversation back to some evangelical "basics." My sessions with Martin were unsettling and fascinating both; on the one hand, I was attracted by his approach to the Scriptures, but on the other I was concerned about the danger of "too much theology" getting in the way of basic Christianity. After we had settled in our chairs, I presented my concern.

"Why should Christians discuss the sorts of doctrines we have been discussing? Shouldn't we just stick to the gospel? Sinful men need to be told that they must be born again, and here we sit, week after week, splitting theological hairs."

Martin chuckled. "To be sure, sinful men need to be told that they must be born again. What would you say if one of them asked you what on earth that meant?"

I stared at him. "Isn't that obvious? It means that men must become Christians."

Martin took a sip of his coffee. "How does one do that?"

I thought for a moment. "Well, the person must repent of his sins, and must put his faith in Jesus Christ, who died on the cross for sinners."

Martin smiled. "Very good—so far. Most Christians would leave the cross out of it altogether—they would say something like 'ask Jesus into your heart,' or 'make a commitment to Christ.' Now what happens after he repents and believes?"

"He is born again."

"Now are you aware that this order—'Repent, believe, and then you will be born again'—is not in the Bible?"

I was actually aware of no such thing, so I shook my head. "What do you mean?"

"How do you know that the biblical order is not, 'You must be born again, in order to repent and believe?'"

I think my mouth was hanging open. I had never heard anything like this before.

"You mean that the new birth is *first?*"

Martin nodded.

"In the order you have assumed, man makes a choice, and then he is born again. But the Bible places the choice regarding the new birth in God's hands, not man's."

"Where?" I asked.

"There are three basic arguments from Scripture for this. The first is how the Spirit's work is described; the second is the nature of *birth*; and the third would be express statements of Scripture to this effect."

I nodded. "Okay, let's start with the first."

He had me turn to John 3:7-8, and I read, *Do not marvel that I said to you, 'You must be born again.' The wind blows where it wishes, and you hear the sound of it, but cannot tell where it comes from and where it goes. So is everyone who is born of the Spirit.* I looked up.

Martin said, "Would you agree that it is fairly common for Christians to evangelize by telling people *how* to be born again?"

"Certainly. Isn't that what evangelism is?"

"No. Evangelism is preaching the death of Christ for sinners, and the necessity of repentance and belief. Telling people how to be born again is like telling people how to understand where the wind comes from, and where it is going. The new birth is *mysterious*—it is the work of the Spirit of God, not the work of man."

"So you are saying that the new birth cannot be controlled by men."

"Yes. I am saying that the wind blows where *He* pleases."

"What must men do then?"

"They must repent and believe on the Lord Jesus Christ."

"So repentance and belief are what the man contributes?"

"In a way. It is the *man* who repents and believes, but the Spirit has made that repentance and belief possible by giving the sinner a new heart through regeneration. So, for example, repentance is described as something men do in Acts 26:20, but it is also seen as a gift from God in 2 Timothy 2:25. In contrast, the new birth is *never* described as anything done by man. It is always shown as the imperial work of God."

"You mentioned the nature of birth. What did you mean by that?"

"Jesus taught that the new birth is necessary. From this, many have falsely concluded that it is a command to be obeyed by us. But 'be born' is a passive verb, not active. 'Repent' and 'believe' are active."

"What does that mean?"

"It means that those who are born again are *recipients*. A birth is not something one volunteers for; it is something that happens to him."

"Can you illustrate?"

"Sure. I was in the Navy for four years, and I am a Spenser. I joined the Navy (voluntarily) and my family (not voluntarily). When Jesus compared the start of the Christian life to a birth, which type of joining did He have in mind?"

"The second, I guess," I said reluctantly.

"And which type of joining is presented in most modern evangelism?"

"The first." I didn't know why I felt so uneasy.

"Exactly. One of the major problems we have in the church today is the result of well-meaning but unbiblical *recruiters*, instead of biblical *evangelists*. We have even fallen to the point where we have borrowed, on a large scale, techniques of recruitment from the world."

"How would you summarize this point about the verb 'be born'?"

"By saying that if the new birth is what many describe it to be, there is no way to express in the language of birth what is happening. Birth would be an extremely clumsy metaphor for what is happening. How does one birth himself?"

I turned to the next point. "You said that there were several verses that make your point about the new birth."

Martin nodded. "Turn to James 1:18. Why don't you read it out loud?"

So I read. *"Of His own will He brought us forth by the word of truth, that we might be a kind of firstfruits of His creatures."*

Martin said, "Notice it does not say, 'Of *our* own will He brought us forth by the word of truth. . . .'"

"Where is the other passage you had in mind?"

"John 1:12-13."

I turned the pages slowly, thinking hard.

But as many as received Him, to them He gave the right to become children of God, even to those who believe in His name: who were born, not of blood, nor of the will of the flesh, nor of the will of man, but of God.

I looked at Martin. "Do you believe there are *no* legitimate questions about what you are saying?"

He laughed. "I would have to be an insufferable coxcomb to say something like that. Someone could say, for example, that some passive verbs can be obeyed by us—'be filled with the Spirit'—and he could maintain that God gives the right to become His children to those who received Him *because* they received Him. But of course I believe such objections, while reasonable, can still be answered."

"There is one thing I still don't understand," I said. "I began by asking whether or not we are splitting theological hairs in our discussions. What practical difference does this all make? I mean, an average non-Christian isn't going to know whether the man preaching to him believes what you are saying or not. So why bother with it? Why don't we just preach the gospel?"

"To say that the non-Christian could not tell the difference is not to say there is no difference."

"What does that mean?"

"Does this make any difference to the *evangelist*? How he
prays, prepares, preaches?"

"What difference could it make?"

"The two preachers have a completely different understanding of their respective tasks. The one believes himself
to be going to the sick, supplied by God with the proper medicine, and his task is to persuade the patients to take the
medicine. The other man is going, like Ezekiel, to preach in
a graveyard."

"Ezekiel?"

"The Lord told him to prophesy to a valley full of dry
bones. I dare say that Ezekiel did so with the full knowledge
that if something were to happen it would have to be the
result of the Spirit's work. It certainly would not be because
of anything Ezekiel did in his own power."

"But all evangelists know that God must empower
them. . . ."

"Yes, *but to do what*? The one seeks to raise conscious-
ness, while the other seeks to raise the dead. All godly evangelists seek to be dependent upon God in the performance of
their task; but their respective theologies will determine their
understanding of that task. Believe me, I have preached the
gospel both ways, and I know the difference it makes."

I scratched my chin thoughtfully. "So you are saying that
Calvinism will result in powerful evangelism. . . ."

"No. And please don't call it Calvinism."

I laughed. "I can't talk about it without words. What do
you want me to call it?"

"Well, we are talking about the new birth. Let's call it
the new birth."

"Okay, okay. Why did you say 'No'?"

"There have been many Christians with an accurate understanding of the gospel who have done little or nothing
with it. There have been others who, like Apollos, have done

a lot with a deficient understanding."

"So this means. . . ."

"It means that if a man is empowered by the Spirit of God, more use will be made of him if he has an accurate understanding of the new birth." Martin grinned. "People who compare George Whitefield with John Wesley are be-ing, shall we say, unscientific? The real question is whether Wesley would have been more powerful had he understood this, and whether Whitefield would have been less powerful had he not. And these questions cannot be answered through historical study; half of the comparision you must make didn't happen. Consequently we are driven to the Scriptures to settle the matter."

"Right," I said, "Back to the Scriptures."

I sat silently for a few moments, and then got up to go.

"Thanks," I said.

Martin nodded. "And as you read, don't forget to *submit* to what you read."

"I think I have been learning what you mean by that. It makes a big difference. See you next week."

Texts on Regeneration

2 Corinthians 3:6
Who also made us sufficient as ministers of the new covenant, not of the letter but of the Spirit; for the letter kills,
but *the Spirit gives life.*

1 Peter 1:2
Elect according to the foreknowledge of God the Father,
in sanctification of the Spirit, for obedience and sprinkling of
the blood of Jesus Christ. . . .

John 3:5-6
Jesus answered, 'Most assuredly, I say to you, unless one
is born of water *and the Spirit,* he cannot enter the kingdom
of God. That which is born of the flesh is flesh, and *that which
is born of the Spirit is spirit.'*

Titus 3:5
Not by works of righteousness which we have done, but
according to His mercy He saved us, *through the washing of
regeneration and renewing of the Holy Spirit.* . . .

Acts 5:31
Him God has exalted to His right hand to be Prince and
Savior, *to give repentance to Israel and forgiveness of sins.*

Acts 11:18
When they heard these things they became silent; and
they glorified God, saying, 'Then God has also *granted* to the
Gentiles *repentance* to life.'

Acts 13:48
Now when the Gentiles heard this, they were glad and
glorified the word of the Lord. *And as many as had been appointed to eternal life believed.*

Acts 16:14

Now a certain woman named Lydia heard us. She was a seller of purple from the city of Thyatira, who worshiped God. *The Lord opened her heart to heed* the things spoken by Paul.

2 Timothy 2:25-26

In humility correcting those who are in opposition, *if God perhaps will grant them repentance*, so that they may know the truth, and that they may come to their senses and escape the snare of the devil, having been taken captive by him to do his will.

John 6:37

All that the Father gives Me *will come to Me*, and the one who comes to Me I will by no means cast out.

Romans 1:6-7

Among whom you also are *the called* of Jesus Christ; to all who are in Rome, beloved of God, *called to be saints.* . . .

Romans 8:30

Moreover whom He predestined, these He also *called*; whom He called, these He also justified; and whom He justified, these He also glorified.

Romans 9:24

Even us *whom He called*, not of the Jews only, but also of the Gentiles?

1 Corinthians 1:2

To the church of God which is at Corinth, to those who are sanctified in Christ Jesus, *called to be saints*, with all who in every place call on the name of Jesus Christ our Lord, both theirs and ours. . . .

1 Corinthians 1:9

God is faithful, by whom you were *called into the fellowship* of His Son, Jesus Christ our Lord.

1 Corinthians 1:23-31

But we preach Christ crucified, to the Jews a stumbling block and to the Greeks foolishness, but to those who are *called*, both Jews and Greeks, Christ the power of God and the wisdom of God.

Because the foolishness of God is wiser than men, and the weakness of God is stronger than men.

For you see your *calling*, brethren, that not many wise according to the flesh, not many mighty, not many noble, are *called*.

But God has *chosen* the foolish things of the world to put to shame the wise, and God has *chosen* the weak things of the world to put to shame the things which are mighty; and the base things of the world and the things which are despised God has *chosen*, and the things which are not, to bring to nothing the things that are, *that no flesh should glory in His presence*.

But of Him you are in Christ Jesus, who became for us wisdom from God—and righteousness and sanctification and redemption—that, as it is written, 'He who glories, let him glory in the Lord.'

Galatians 1:15-16

But when it pleased God, who separated me from my mother's womb and *called* me through His grace, *to reveal His Son in me*, that I might preach Him among the Gentiles, I did not immediately confer with flesh and blood. . .

Ephesians 4:4

There is one body and one Spirit, just as you were *called* in one hope of your *calling*. . .

2 Timothy 1:9

Who *saved us and called us* with a holy calling, not according to our works, but according to His own purpose and grace which was *given to us in Christ Jesus before time began.*

Jude 1

To those who are *called*, sanctified by God the Father, and preserved in Jesus Christ. . . .

1 Peter 1:15

But as He who *called* you is holy, you also be holy in all your conduct.

1 Peter 5:10

But may the God of all grace, *who called us* to His eternal glory by Christ Jesus, after you have suffered a while, perfect, establish, strengthen, and settle you.

2 Peter 1:3

As His divine power has given to us all things that pertain to life and godliness, through the knowledge of Him *who called us* by glory and virtue. . . .

James 1:18

Of His own will He brought us forth by the word of truth, that we might be a kind of firstfruits of His creatures.

twelve

Death in Sin

"I must confess," I said, "that I have talked with another pastor about our conversations."

Martin laughed. "There is nothing there to confess, surely!"

"Well, he sure didn't agree with what you are saying."

"That's fine too. Did he agree with the Bible though?"

It was my turn to laugh. "That was a little less clear than his disagreement with *you*. But he did say one thing that I was wondering about."

"What was it?"

"He said that Calvinists believe in something they call *total depravity*. He said they have a very low opinion of man."

"The second part is true enough. But the first phrase he used–*total depravity*–is a good example of something we have addressed before. There is a problem with terminology here. What comes to mind with the phrase *total depravity*?"

"It makes me think of the bottom pit of Hell."

"Right. Total depravity sounds like *absolute* depravity. The phrase makes it sound as though there is nothing good about unregenerate men, and that they are the moral equivalent of utterly corrupt demons."

"So what does the phrase refer to?"

"It refers to man's total inability with regard to his own salvation. He is incapacitated by his own sin in such a way that he cannot contribute to his own salvation in any way, shape or form."

"But he is not totally and finally wicked?"

"Obviously not. Non-Christians can do many things which are in themselves good. There is no merit for them in this, however; they only do such things because they are restrained from evil by God's common grace, and even the good they do is done for selfish motives, and not for the glory of God. Even so, many such non-Christians make fine next-door neighbors."

"I see. So then what is the biblical basis for saying that man is totally unable to contribute to his own salvation?"

"It is very simple. The Bible teaches that unregenerate men are dead in their sin. This is in contrast to the common evangelical picture of men as *sick* in their sin."

"Where does the Bible teach this?"

"I'll give you several passages to consider now, and later on, I'll give you a longer list to study at your leisure."

"Fine."

"The first is in Ephesians 2:1. *And you He made alive, who were dead in trespasses and sins. . . .*"

I quickly flipped to the passage, and looked it over. I looked up. "But unregenerate men can think, believe, laugh, walk, move . . . in what sense are they dead?"

"The Bible does not teach that men are dead in every respect. It simply teaches that with respect to spiritual things, they are dead. Flesh, because it is alive, can give birth to flesh, and does. But it cannot give birth to spirit."

"So you are saying that men are *spiritually dead*, but not dead physically and mentally?"

"Yes. And I am saying this because the Bible teaches it. Look at Colossians 2:13."

I turned to the passage and read aloud. *"And you, being dead in your trespasses and the uncircumcision of your flesh, He has made alive together with Him. . . ."* I trailed off. "It seems pretty clear."

"It is very clear. Now, what can we say about death?"

"I don't get you."

"What can a dead man do?"

"Of course, nothing."

"Right. Was the resurrection of Lazarus a cooperative effort between Lazarus and Christ? Or was it the power of Christ alone?"

"Obviously, it was the power of Christ alone."

"So when the Bible teaches that men are dead with regard to spiritual things, then if those men are made alive, it must be because of a unilateral action on God's part?"

"I guess so."

"Theologians call this concept *monergism*. God, and God alone, does the spiritual work upon the dead sinner. Those who believe that this spiritual work is a cooperative effort are proponents of *synergism*—God and man working together."

"I see. But what difference does this make? Both sides would say that men need God."

"Yes, but there is a vast difference between a God who helps out and a God who resurrects. There is considerable difference between preaching in a hospital ward and preaching in a graveyard. If a man can believe with his old heart, *he doesn't need a new one.*"

"Surely death is not the only picture the Bible gives us of the condition of sinful men, is it?"

"Certainly not. But it is a telling image, is it not? Another telling picture is the one of slavery, and it also communicates the concept of total inability."

"Can you give me an example of this?"

"Sure. In Romans 6. I think it is around verse 21?"

I turned to the passage, and ran my finger down the page. "20," I said. "This whole section is about slavery. But verse 20 says, *For when you were slaves of sin, you were free in regard to righteousness.*"

"So before these Roman Christians were saved, they took their orders from sin, not from righteousness?"

"Correct."

"Now what will Master Sin tell this slave to do when the

slave is confronted with the righteousness of the gospel?"

"The master will tell his slave to disregard the gospel."

"And the slave will remain a slave unless. . . ?"

"I see it! Unless someone stronger comes and binds the master."

"Right. And that stronger one is the Lord. Not the slave. And the sense of liberation which results is put well in one of my favorite hymns—written by someone whose poetry was sounder than his theology. 'My *chains fell off, my heart was free, I rose, went forth, and followed thee.*'"

I laughed. "It makes so much sense. God raises me from the dead, and *then* I live. God strikes off my chains, and *then* I go free. God restores my sight, and *then* I see."

"That's it. Dead men don't raise themselves, slaves to sin don't free themselves, blind men don't give themselves sight, and so forth. What they receive, they receive as a *gift.*"

"Got it. One thing still puzzles me though."

"And what is that?"

"Why haven't I seen this before? I believed bits and pieces of it as long as I can remember, but I never put it all together."

"I have met many Christians just like that. I used to be just that way myself. It seems to be fairly common. They believe in, and comfort themselves with, one side of the coin. They are also careful always to keep the other side of the coin table-side down."

I got up to go. "Well, I guess I'll be back next week. You are still making sense to me."

Martin laughed. "Next week then."

Texts on the Condition of Man

Ephesians 2:1-3
And you *He made alive*, who were *dead* in trespasses and sins, in which you once walked according to the course of this world, according to the prince of the power of the air, the spirit who now works in the *sons of disobedience*, among whom also we all once conducted ourselves in the lusts of our flesh, fulfilling the desires of the flesh and of the mind, and were *by nature children of wrath*, just as the others.

Jeremiah 17:9
The heart is *deceitful above all things*, and *desperately wicked*; who can know it?

Romans 8:7-8
Because the carnal mind is *enmity against God*; for it is not subject to the law of God, *nor indeed can be*. So then, those who are in the flesh *cannot please God*.

Genesis 2:16-17
And the Lord God commanded the man, saying, 'Of every tree of the garden you may freely eat; but of the tree of the knowledge of good and evil you shall not eat, for in the day that you eat of it *you shall surely die.*'

Romans 5:12
Therefore, just as through one man sin entered the world, and *death* through sin, and thus *death* spread to all men, *because all sinned.* . . .

Psalm 58:3
The wicked are estranged from the womb; They go astray as soon as they are born, speaking lies.

Genesis 8:21
And the Lord smelled a soothing aroma. Then the Lord

said in His heart, 'I will never again curse the ground for man's sake, although the imagination of man's heart is *evil from his youth. . . .*'

Mark 7:21-23

For from within, *out of the heart of men*, proceed evil thoughts, adulteries, fornications, murders, thefts, covetousness, wickedness, deceit, licentiousness, an evil eye, blasphemy, pride, foolishness. All these evil things come *from within* and defile a man.

John 3:19-21

And this is the condemnation, that the light has come into the world, and *men loved darkness rather than light*, because their deeds were evil. For everyone practicing evil hates the light and does not come to the light, lest his deeds should be exposed. But he who does the truth comes to the light, that his deeds may be clearly seen, *that they have been done in God.*

1 Corinthians 2:14

But the natural man *does not receive* the things of the Spirit of God, for they are *foolishness to him*; nor *can* he know them, because they are spiritually discerned.

Romans 3:9-12

What then? Are we better than they? Not at all. For we have previously charged both Jews and Greeks that they are *all under sin*. As it is written:
'There is *none* righteous, *no, not one*;
There is *none* who understands;
There is *none* who seeks after God.
They have *all* gone out of the way;
They have together become unprofitable;
There is *none* who does good, *no, not one.*'

Jeremiah 13:23

Can the Ethiopian change his skin or the leopard its spots? *Then may you also do good* who are accustomed to do evil.

Matthew 7:18

A good tree cannot bear bad fruit, *nor can a bad tree bear good fruit.*

John 6:44

No one can come to Me unless the Father who sent Me drew him; and I will raise him up at the last day.

John 6:65

And He said, 'Therefore I have said to you that *no one can come to Me* unless it has been granted to him by My Father.'

_____ thirteen _____

All Men?

"Well," I said, "I did what you said to do."

"And what was that?" Martin asked.

"I've been reading my Bible . . . a lot. It has answered a lot of questions. But it has raised some others."

"Of course. Where have you been reading?"

"I just finished the book of Romans. I don't mean to be irreverent, but at first glance it looks like Paul couldn't make up his mind."

Martin laughed. "What do you mean?"

"I mean that chapters eight through eleven look like they were written by Calvin himself. But chapter five looks like John Wesley wrote it. My reading has confirmed much of what you have said. . . but it has unsettled other aspects of what you have taught me."

He laughed again. "Let's look at it in detail then. But first, we must begin with a fundamental assumption."

"What is that?"

"It is that God's Word does not contradict itself. Whatever the teaching of chapter five, it is in harmony with chapters eight and following. Fair enough?"

"Fair enough."

We had both turned to chapter five, and sat silently reading it. When we were done, Martin asked me, "What does this say which you feel is not consistent with what I've been saying?"

"Before I answer, would you mind doing me a favor?"

"Not at all."

"Could you answer my questions out of *this* passage, and not out of the later chapters? I already know what they say."

"No problem."

"Well, then, here's the problem. Paul appears to be arguing that the first Adam sinned in such a way as to bring death to all men—every last one. Paul then says that the second Adam, Christ, has the same kind of impact on all men—every last one—only His impact is beneficial. How is it possible to say that *all* and *many* are referring to different groups of people? Paul seems to be saying that Adam had a destructive impact on every person, and Christ had a beneficial impact on every person. Isn't that the simplest way to handle the passage?"

"No."

"Excuse me?"

"I said no."

"All right," I said. "How come?"

"We must identify the *all* and the *many* by what this passage predicates of them."

"What do you mean?"

"We may learn the identity of these people by how they are described. Let's begin by identifying a problem with how you are understanding it."

"Well, okay."

"Read through the passage aloud, and every time the words *all* or *many* occur, insert a phrase which makes your understanding explicit. Use the phrase *all men without exception*."

"What good will that do?"

"Trust me. It will reveal something."

"Okay. Here goes." And I began to read.

"Therefore, just as through one man sin entered the world, and death through sin, and thus death spread to all men *without exception*, because all men *without exception* sinned—(For until the law sin was in the world, but sin is not imputed when there is no law.

"Nevertheless death reigned from Adam to Moses, even over those who had not sinned according to the likeness of the transgression of Adam, who is a type of Him who was to come.

"But the free gift is not like the offense. For if by the one man's offense all men *without exception* died, much more the grace of God and the gift by the grace of the one Man, Jesus Christ, abounded to all men *without exception*.

"And the gift is not like that which came through the one who sinned. For the judgment which came from one offense resulted in condemnation, but the free gift which came from many offenses resulted in justification.

"For if by the one man's offense death reigned through the one, much more those who receive abundance of grace and of the gift of righteousness will reign in life through the One, Jesus Christ.)

"Therefore, as through one man's offense judgment came to all men *without exception*, resulting in condemnation, even so through one Man's righteous act the free gift came to all men *without exception*, resulting in justification of life.

"For as by one man's disobedience all men *without exception* were made sinners, so also by one Man's obedience all men *without exception* will be made righteous.

"Moreover the law entered that the offense might abound. But where sin abounded, grace abounded much more, so that as sin reigned in death, even so grace might reign through righteousness to eternal life through Jesus Christ our Lord."

I looked up. "Some of that didn't sound right."

"Exactly. There is a reason for that. If Paul is referring to all men without exception throughout the passage, then what must we say? One: Death comes to all men without exception. No problem. Two: All men without exception are sinners. No problem here either. Three: All men without exception die as a result of Adam's transgression. True. Four:

Therefore God's grace and gift through Jesus Christ abounded to all men without exception. May be a problem, but nothing certain yet. Five: Judgment falls on all men without exception. True. Six: All men without exception *receive justification of life.* Here is an immense problem. Paul tells us a few pages later that those whom God justified, He glorified. Are all men without exception justified? Are all men without exception glorified? 7) All men without exception were made sinners. That's true. 8) All men without exception *will be made righteous.* Now unless we are prepared to embrace universalism, which we cannot do because of what we are taught elsewhere, the *all* and the *many* cannot be talking about the same group of people."

I sat staring at the page. I felt as though I had been hit by a rock. I looked up.

"I see." I looked back at the passage. "For the evangelical arguing against the exhaustive sovereignty of God, this passage proves way too much."

"Exactly. He wants *potential* universality, and there is nothing potential in this passage at all. The consequences of the sin of Adam flowed downstream to all his descendants. Without exception. As it happens, that is the entire human race."

"There is no potential in what the second Adam does either. It flows downstream the same way."

"Right. In the same way."

"But not to the entire human race."

Martin nodded his head. "Because. . . ?"

"Because of what this passage says about Christ's descendants. All of them receive justification to life, and all of them will be made righteous. Paul is therefore not talking about those who do not receive justification to life; he is not talking about those who remain unrighteous."

"You've got it."

I thought of something, and turned to the passage to read again.

"Therefore, just as through one man sin entered the

world, and death through sin, and thus death spread to *all Adam's descendants*, because *all Adam's descendants* sinned— (For until the law sin was in the world, but sin is not imputed when there is no law.

"Nevertheless death reigned from Adam to Moses, even over those who had not sinned according to the likeness of the transgression of Adam, who is a type of Him who was to come.

"But the free gift is not like the offense. For if by the one man's offense *all Adam's descendants* died, much more the grace of God and the gift by the grace of the one Man, Jesus Christ, abounded to *all Christ's descendants*.

"And the gift is not like that which came through the one who sinned. For the judgment which came from one offense resulted in condemnation, but the free gift which came from many offenses resulted in justification.

"For if by the one man's offense death reigned through the one, much more those who receive abundance of grace and of the gift of righteousness will reign in life through the One, Jesus Christ.)

"Therefore, as through one man's offense judgment came to *all Adam's descendants*, resulting in condemnation, even so through one Man's righteous act the free gift came to *all Christ's descendants*, resulting in justification of life.

"For as by one man's disobedience *all Adam's descendants* were made sinners, so also by one Man's obedience *all Christ's descendants* will be made righteous.

"Moreover the law entered that the offense might abound. But where sin abounded, grace abounded much more, so that as sin reigned in death, even so grace might reign through righteousness to eternal life through Jesus Christ our Lord."

"Makes more sense, doesn't it?"

"A lot more sense. But, may I be the devil's advocate for a moment?"

"Certainly."

"What justification can we have for just inserting *Christ's descendants*, and *Adam's descendants*, wherever we feel like it? That doesn't seem like sober exegesis."

"It seems like trifling with the text at first glance. Or mangling the text to save our system. But there are several things to remember. We didn't go hunting for alternative meanings for *all* and *many* just for grins. There was a reason in the passage for doing so. To take those words at their *prima facie* meaning results in absurdities. All men without exception are justified? All men without exception will be made righteous?"

"You said there were several reasons?"

"Yes. It is very clear in the passage that Paul is contrasting two *Adams*. These two Adams, by definition, are the representative heads of their respective descendants. It makes good *contextual* sense to understand the *all* and the *many* as the respective descendants of the respective Adams."

"Is this the only passage where this is taught?"

"No. And that is another thing we can bring to bear on this discussion. Paul teaches about the two Adams in 1 Corinthians 15 as well. There this distinction is made explicit."

I had turned to the chapter. "What verse?"

"Verses 22-23."

Martin sat back in his chair while I read.

For as in Adam all die, even so in Christ all shall be made alive. But each one in his own order: Christ the firstfruits, afterward those who are Christ's at His coming.

I looked up.

"Where do all die?"

I looked back at the text.

"In Adam."

"Where are all made alive?"

"In Christ."

"That phrase—*in Christ*—does it ring any bells for you? How does Paul use it?"

"Paul uses it to describe Christians."

"Right. Now, in verse 22, those who are made alive are described by the word *all*."

"Yes."

"How are they described in verse 23?"

I looked again. "It is made explicit—*those who are Christ's.*"

"Exactly. In Adam, all Adam's descendants die, and in Christ, all who belong to Him live."

"Boy, this is a mouthful."

Martin nodded.

"And it takes some getting used to. Take your time."

fourteen

Is Anything Too Hard for God?

"It seems to me," I said, "that there is a philosophical problem here."

"What do you mean?" Martin waited.

"How would you respond to the charge that your beliefs about God and His exhaustive sovereignty are a *philosophical* conception of God? You know, God must be the greatest conceivable being, perfect in every way. Because of this any 'free will' on the part of man would detract from His perfections, so therefore exhaustive sovereignty is a necessity. I have been told that all this stuff was brought into Christianity by Augustine, who got it from Greek philosophy."

"Well, I guess I would ask for a source."

"Beg pardon?"

"I would ask for a source. I have seen the charge too—many times. I have not seen it documented. And, when you come to think about it, the charge is kind of funny."

"How so?"

"Well, the ancient Greeks were divided among themselves. Some of them thought that everything was frozen. Motion was an illusion, all was immutable. Others thought that everything was flux, and always changing. You can't step into the same river twice. That sort of thing."

"Why is that funny? I must not get the joke."

"Christians who hold that God is immutable are charged with importing the idea from Greek philosophy. Of course, those who hold that God is *not* immutable could be charged with the same thing, Greek philosophers being on both sides of the issue and all."

I smiled. "So where do you get the idea, for example, that if God purposes or intends, or wills something, then that something must come to pass?"

Martin leaned forward. "It is very simple. I studied Greek philosophy thirty years ago in college. I read my Bible every day."

"Oh," I said. "Where does the Bible teach that God's purposes are unchangeable?"

"First allow me to make a distinction."

"Shoot."

"That there is a 'will of God' which can be thwarted is beyond dispute. God says, 'You shall not steal,' and that state-ment is an expression of His will. But still, sinful people steal all the time, transgressing His will. We are concerned here with His *eternal purpose*. Within that purpose, there has never been, and never will be, a plan B. What God intends to do is always done."

"I think I understand," I said. I had my Bible out on my lap.

"Look first at Ephesians 3:11. . . . *according to his eternal purpose which he accomplished in Christ Jesus our Lord*. God's purpose here is described as eternal."

I nodded, while scribbling in my notebook.

"Now turn to Ephesians 1:11. *In him we were also chosen, having been predestined according to the plan of him who works out everything in conformity with the purpose of his will*. . . My point here is not the reference to predestination, but rather to the fact that God works out *everything* according to His purpose. Consequently, His purposes do not need to change."

I nodded again. "Go on."

"The prophet Isaiah, in 55:11, said . . . *so is my word that goes out from my mouth: It will not return to me empty, but will accomplish what I desire and achieve the purpose for which I sent it*. What God intends for His word to accomplish, it will accomplish. In another place, chapter 46, verse 10, Isaiah says, *I make known the end from the beginning, from ancient times, what is still to come. I say: My purpose will stand, and I will do all that I please."*

I grinned. "Could you give me a verse that addresses it a little more plainly?"

"How about the lesson Job learned? In 42:1-2, it says, *Then Job replied to the Lord, 'I know that you can do all things; no plan of yours can be thwarted.'"*

I went back to writing.

"Proverbs 19:21 says, *Many are the plans in a man's heart, but it is the Lord's purpose that prevails.*"

I had turned to the passage. "So it does."

"And then in Numbers 23:19 we learn that *God is not a man, that he should lie, nor a son of man, that he should change his mind. Does he speak and then not act? Does he promise and not fulfill?* These are rhetorical questions, and the answer is no."

I looked up. "This all seems pretty clear."

"It does. In Daniel 4:35, even the the great pagan king of Babylon had a better grasp of this than many Christians do: *All the peoples of the earth are regarded as nothing. He does as He pleases with the powers of heaven and the peoples of the earth. No one can hold back His hand or say to Him: 'What have you done?'*"

"It seems that to deny this is to say that certain things are too hard for God."

"Right. And nothing is too hard for God. Jeremiah 32:27 says, *I am the Lord, the God of all mankind. Is anything too hard for Me?*"

"I don't think so," I said.

Martin leaned back. "Neither do I. In Matthew 19:26, it says, *Jesus looked at them and said, 'With man this is impossible, but with God all things are possible.'* If I got these ideas from Greek philosophy, I wonder where Jesus got them?"

_____ fifteen _____

Two Kinds of Freedom

"Why is there so much confusion on this issue?" I asked.

Martin thought for a moment. "One of the problems we face in discussing this issue is the problem of keeping categories distinct. The sovereignty of God relates to human freedom on two different levels."

"Okay," I said. "What is the first level?"

"The first level is a _metaphysical_ problem."

"What do you mean?"

"When a man, Christian or not, walks into Baskin-Robbins, is he _free_ to select any one of the thirty-one flavors? In other words, is man, _as creature_, free?"

"All right. What is the second level?"

"The second level is the problem concerning morality. Does a non-Christian man have the freedom to avoid sin? Can he choose not to? In other words, is man, _as sinner_, free?"

I nodded my head. The two questions were entirely different.

Martin went on. "With regard to the first, the Bible teaches that man is free to go here or go there, do this or do that, marry this woman or that one, and so forth. He is a responsible agent, precisely because God gave him that responsibility. God is Creator, and has given his creatures a creaturely freedom. Now of course the choices we make as creatures are not outside God's providential government of the world; they are included in it. God ordains what choices will be made, and he also ordains that they will be free choices. So the question here is how we may reconcile the creaturely freedom of man with the absolute freedom of God in His government of the universe."

"So are you saying that God governs and controls the choices we make as creatures?"

"Certainly. And how this can be understood at the same time we affirm the genuine creaturely freedom of man is a *metaphysical* problem."

"It sure is," I said. "Are you going to come back to it?"

Martin nodded, but then added, "The point to be remembered here is that this creaturely freedom can not only be reconciled with God's providential control, but could not exist without it. Such creaturely freedom is the only freedom *possible* for creatures. So in a decision on whether to turn right or left, we, as creatures, are in the same position that Adam was in before the Fall. God was God then, just as He is now. Human beings, fallen or not, have always been creatures. We have freedom to choose, but freedom is not based on the contingency of the future event."

"Okay. What about the area of morality?"

"In *this* realm, the realm of morality and ethics, the Bible teaches that man is a slave to his sins, and can do nothing about it. Because he still has his creaturely freedom, he may choose vodka or gin, this whore or that one, this kind of sin or that kind of sin. But even though he retains his creaturely freedom, he *cannot* escape the bondage of sin."

"Why can he not escape it?"

"Because he cannot escape what he is, and what he loves. He *is* a sinner, and he *loves* sin."

I thought for a moment, and Martin continued.

"It is at this level that many have their most difficult problem with the sovereignty of God. Why does God give repentance to Smith and not to Jones? We have come to that subset of God's eternal decree which we call election. It is here that we most desperately want to reconcile God's choices with man's freedom. But it is also here that the task becomes impossible, for the simple reason that at this point man has *no freedom*."

"What!"

"No freedom. How can we reconcile a non-existent attribute of man (the freedom to make a correct moral choice) with the sovereignty of God? There is nothing there to reconcile. When God calls a man, He *creates* freedom. When we become Christians, God is not violating our moral freedom—He is creating it. Where the Spirit of the Lord is, there is liberty."

"All right," I said dubiously.

"The new creation is not the result of a partnership between the will of man and the will of God. It is the result of the work of God alone. But once God has done his work, the work *is* done. The result is a holy people—people who are able to do the right thing. The result of God's work is moral liberty where none existed before."

"Why is this distinction important?"

"Because in the debate over free will this distinction has been frequently muddled. It makes a difference whether we are considering man as creature, or man as sinner. It makes a difference whether we consider God as Creator or God as Savior. Our Creator gives us responsible lives to live, all within the context of his purpose and plan. Our Savior gives freedom where there was slavery, and life where there was death."

"So you believe the Bible teaches this distinction?"

"Certainly. Distinguishing our relation to God as Savior and God as Creator does help us to understand the issue a little more clearly, but the pride of man still reacts to both truths. For some, the offense against logic is too great. They consider the sovereignty of God and the responsibility of man to be irreconcilables. To resolve the problem, some say that God does not exercise His liberty in this way. Others resolve the problem by saying that man is not really responsible. Both accuse the one who wants to hold both positions in biblical balance of being illogical."

"But isn't there a logical problem with it?"

"How can there be? We can have no logical problem when we do not have all the premises. And the Bible expressly says that we do not and cannot have them."

"Where?" I asked.

Martin counted them off on his fingers. "In Deuteronomy 29:29, Psalm 139:1-6, Romans 9:20-21, and Romans 11:33-36. We do not have all the premises, and therefore there are aspects to this discussion which we cannot understand. But God does have all the premises, and the problem of human freedom and divine sovereignty most certainly does not keep *Him* up nights."

"So what does this mean?"

"It means that there is no reason why we should be forced to choose between two positions, when both are equally biblical. Suppose for a moment that the debate concerned light instead of free will."

"Light?"

Martin took a sip from his coffee. "Uh-huh. We are confronted in the Bible with the statement, 'And God said, "Let there be light."' Immediately, we foolishly divide into two parties. The one says, 'See, here is the light. Why should we believe that God created it?' The opposing group says, 'God said there should be light, therefore there is no real light.' If neither alternative makes sense to you, that is good."

"Well, I'm not sure it is good. I don't get what you are driving at."

"The Bible teaches that God creates light in our hearts. In 2 Corinthians 4:6, it says, *For God, who said, 'Let light shine out of darkness,' made His light shine in our hearts to give us the light of the knowledge of the glory of God in the face of Christ.* Confronted with this, we divide into two parties."

"What are the two groups?"

"The one says, 'Jones has light in his heart. Therefore God did not put it there.' The other says, 'God put it there, therefore *Jones* does not really have light.' Neither option makes sense, and neither is biblical."

"Go on."

"God does not decree light and then *pretend* there is light. He decrees light, and there is light. When God decrees light in the heart of Jones, *God* is the one who decrees, and therefore it is *Jones* who believes. God does not decree optical illusions."

"So you are saying that the decree of God is not, 'I will repent and make it look like Jones did.' It is, 'Jones will repent.'"

Martin nodded. "Because of this gracious gift, Jones repents. There are some who point to the indisputable repentance of Jones (it wasn't *Smith* who repented), and conclude that God could not have given it. Others point to the biblically indisputable fact that God gives repentance, and conclude that Jones doesn't really have it. The biblical position is that Jones has it *because* God gives it."

I got up to go. "I think I have enough to chew on for this week."

_____ sixteen _____

God in the Dock

"I think I know what you are going to say," I said.

"Is it because I have said it before?" Martin asked.

"Well, yes, but the subject keeps coming up in my mind. It won't go away. How can all this be reconciled with the justice of God?"

"What do you mean? What is there to reconcile?"

"If God totally controls everything, and sin exists, doesn't this make Him the author of sin? I have one friend who told me that whenever he thinks all this might be true, it makes him want to blaspheme. Something must be wrong with this somewhere."

"There is certainly a question we can address in this, but before we do, consider a moment the attitude of your friend."

"What do you mean?"

"If this teaching is false, his response is inappropriate. He, as a Christian, should be grieved that fellow Christians are teaching such falsehood."

"But what if it is true? That's what bothers him."

"But if it is true, then it must also be lovely. God is the source of all truth, and all beauty. The two are never inconsistent. Truth is sometimes hard, but it is never ugly. And those who want to blaspheme because it strikes them as ugly are simply revealing an ugliness in their own hearts. That reaction is a sin that must be confessed."

"You said there was a question concerning this that we could address?"

"Yes. You said that if God totally controls everything, and sin exists, then this would seem to make Him the author of sin?"

"Correct. It seems to me to be a real problem."

"Before we address it, we should first perhaps consider what an oddity it is."

"*Oddity?*"

"Yes. One group of Christians demands that another group of Christians answer this particular question, while off to the side, non-Christians are demanding that *all* Christians answer the same question."

"You missed me. What question?"

"The question or problem created in our minds by the existence of evil and the omnipotence of God. Why does evil exist? Does it exist because God wants it to, or does it exist against His will?"

"I see. If the former, then how can God be good, and if the latter, how can God be all powerful?"

"Right. Now one group of Christians affirms, with the Bible, that God controls everything. Some Christians react to this, because they don't want to say anything that might reflect poorly on the goodness of God. They then adopt the position that God *allows* evil to happen, without recognizing that this can be interpreted to reflect on the goodness of God to the same extent the other position does."

"Could you illustrate this?"

"Sure. I read in the paper this morning that a little girl was murdered by her mother's live-in boyfriend. Now, as Paul would say, I am going to speak foolishly for a moment. Suppose that we have the right to charge God with wrongdoing. Of what would we accuse Him here?"

"Well, if God controls everything, then He controls this, and if He controls this, we could accuse Him of malice, murder, bloodthirstiness, and so on."

"So if He controls everything, then His goodness is defiled because of the sin of murder."

"Right."

"Now suppose that God does not control everything, but merely allows it. Remember, everything He allows He has the power to stop. He didn't control the murder of the little girl, but He could have stopped it and did not. How could we charge Him now?"

"Well, I guess we could accuse Him of apathy, indifference to suffering, culpable negligence, and so on."

"Very good. Would these sins defile the goodness of God?"

"Yes. Just like the other ones."

I sat in thought for a moment, and then responded.

"But couldn't an advocate of 'God allowing sin' say that He allows it for a very good reason?"

"Sure, but the other side could say the same thing. God controls sin the way He does for a very good reason."

I sat for a moment, stumped. Martin continued. "The reason people accept the view that God allows sin is not because it deals with the question of the problem of evil effectively. It does not, as many non-Christian philosophers have seen very well. The reason people accept this explanation is because of 'the very good reason' God supposedly has for allowing sin."

"What is that 'very good reason'?"

"Free will. Man's free will is, in this view, so important, that God is willing to let little girls be murdered for the sake of it. Beyond that, He is willing for non-Christians never to hear the message of salvation so that the messengers may have free will. People are willing to accept horrendous evil, if that evil exists for the sake of free will."

"What is the 'very good reason' of the other side? Why does evil exist according to the view that God controls everything?"

"God controls everything for His own glory. In the minds of many, this is totally inadequate. What is the glory of God compared to the free will of man?"

"Are you being sarcastic?"

Martin smiled. "A little."

"May I try to summarize what you have said?"

"Please."

"The thing that distinguishes the two positions is not whether God is responsible for the continued existence of evil. All Christians acknowledge that God has the power to prevent evil, but that He, for some reason, does not. And both maintain that He has good reason for doing so."

"Good so far."

"They part company on what this good reason *is*. One says that He will use evil to His glory, and the other says that He permits evil so that men may have free will."

Martin replied, "Almost. I would correct that last statement to say that He permits evil so that *some* men may have free will."

"How is that?"

"If God permits 'free will' to the point of sin, then one of the sinful things a man may do is to take away another's free will—even with regard to spiritual things."

"How could one do that?"

"Doesn't this happen every time a non-Christian is murdered? What happens to the man who is killed before he has a chance to become a Christian? Jones goes off to Hell, so that Smith may have the freedom to shoot his gun however he pleases."

I nodded my head. "Okay. I think I've got it."

"Now do you see how this relates the question of God's secret decrees and God's explicit commands?"

"Well, not really."

"Many times I have had Christians ask me how God could command someone not to do something, and punish him for disobeying, if God in His secret eternal counsels had decreed that the deed be done. They objected to the apparent collision between God's decretive will (requiring the deed), and God's prescriptive will (prohibiting the deed)."

"I still don't see how this relates."

"Many of those who take this line want to say there is no discrepancy between God's decretive will and His prescriptive will. They say the two are the same."

"Oh, I see how it relates then! All Christians must recognize a distinction between the decretive and prescriptive will of God in order to be consistent. Those who say that distinguishing the two is artificial are being inconsistent. The difference between them should not be over *whether* God has a decretive will, but rather what the ground of that decree is."

"You are on the right track."

"All admit that God's prescriptive will is violated every day. God says not to steal, and men steal anyway."

"Right."

"And they all must admit, to be consistent, that God's decretive will is not violated. One says that God decrees free will, even if evil results. The other says that God decrees to use all evil for the sake of His glory. But both agree that what God decrees is done."

"Go on."

"And so the debate should center on which is the biblical ground for God's decrees. Whether or not God's decrees are inconsistent with what He commands is a phony debate—the result of confused definitions. But there is one thing I'd like you to touch on before I go."

"What is that?"

"You said earlier that you were speaking foolishly. Did that have to do with the whole idea of sitting in judgment on God?"

"Right. The whole idea is ludicrous. And it is even more ludicrous to think God may only be hauled into court if the charges are serious enough. If we have the authority to accuse Him, then let us not be timid! We should not only go after His sins of commission, but after sins of omission as well."

"If the pot can accuse the Potter for controlling evil, then why not accuse Him for permitting it?"

"Exactly. But of course the idea of judging God is crazy

on the face of it. I remember a delightfully ironic passage in Luther's *Bondage of the Will*. 'It must be false that God has mercy on whom He will have mercy, and hardens whom He will. He must be brought to order! Rules must be laid down for Him, and He is not to damn any but those who have deserved it by *our* reckoning!' The very idea makes us smile. And if it weren't for the tragedy of many Christians talking this way, it really would be funny."

"You are really starting to make sense to me, I'm afraid. Sins of ommission! Sin against what? or whom?"

"Right. There is sin, but it is that of creatures who refuse to believe what they are told to believe."

"I'm afraid I have been guilty."

"We all have. But there is forgiveness for those who confess it and forsake it."

seventeen

Study and Work

"Look," I said, "I have heard you mention that many Christians don't study their Bibles. Were you saying that anyone who disagrees with you on this question of God's sovereignty hasn't done his homework?"

Martin shook his head. "No, I'm not saying that at all. I'm saying that, in my experience, *most* of them have not."

"But you would agree that there are fine Bible scholars who differ with you on this?"

"That depends on what you mean."

"What do *you* mean?"

"There are men who are fine Christians who do not understand this truth. There are men who are fine scholars who differ with it. But when they dispute this truth, in certain key passages, there is an unfortunate lapse of their scholarship."

"May I play the devil's advocate?"

"Certainly."

"Who are *you* to say what the correct interpretation is? Isn't it arrogant of you to say that you are right and all the others are wrong?"

"It is not a question of whether *I* am right. It is a question of whether God *revealed* this truth in his Word, or not."

"I don't get your point."

"We must not, as Christians, determine whether or not God has revealed something by how many men acknowledge the revelation. The content of the revelation is determined by the careful and laborious study of the text. It is not determined by counting noses. Not even scholarly noses."

"Are you saying that you cannot make a mistake when *you* go to the text?"

"No, certainly not. I have made many mistakes. But I may only acknowledge my error when someone shows me the mistake *from the text.*"

"Now how does this relate to the question of God's exhaustive sovereignty?"

"I have had many Christians tell me I am wrong about all this predestination business. But only a handful of them have ever endeavored to demonstrate the error I am supposed to be making from the text."

"What do the rest of them do?"

"They break down into two basic categories. The first group talks just long enough to establish where the disagreement lies; after that, they avoid any discussion of the issue. Thinking about it discomfits them. The second group will talk about it; indeed, many times they enjoy talking about it. But the authority to which they appeal makes any resolution of the question impossible. Their authority, their court of appeals, is reason, common sense, and armchair philosophy. They will say that *reason* requires us to acknowledge that we have 'free will.' Otherwise, how could God blame us? For who resists His will? This group acknowledges the authority of the Bible—on paper—but does not submit to the *arbitration* of Scripture."

"Why do you think this is?"

"I cannot say; I merely see the results of it. Only God sees the heart. I am not competent to say what obstacles may exist in their hearts, although I do not doubt they are there. It is my business to see to it that there is no obstacle to their understanding in *my* heart."

"What do you mean?"

"I mean any kind of pride, haughtiness, impatience . . . whatever. If there is any of this on my part, it may well be used by God to keep fellow Christians from these wonderful truths. In the providence of God, matters are arranged in the church in such a way that it is possible to stumble your brother."

"Can you give me an example of this from Scripture?"

"Sure. In 2 Timothy 2:25, it assumes that God is the Giver of repentance. When a man repents, he is the recipient of a *gift*."

I had looked the passage up. "Well, it sure looks that way."

"Now many Christians deny that repentance is a gift of God. In a discussion with such a person, what do you think the temptation is?"

I grinned. "To beat them over the head with this verse?"

"Exactly. Now back up and read the previous verse, this verse, and the verse after."

I looked down. *And a servant of the Lord must not quarrel but be gentle to all, able to teach, patient, in humility correcting those who are in opposition, if God perhaps will grant them repentance, so that they may know the truth, and that they may come to their senses and escape the snare of the devil, having been taken captive by him to do his will.*

I glanced up again. "But isn't this talking about a debate with a non-Christian?"

"Yes, it is. And if we ought to correct *unbelievers* with such humility, what should our demeanor be toward brothers?"

"Got it," I said.

"Now notice that the behavior of the one who knows the truth is connected with the possible change of heart of the one listening, if God is gracious and so wills it."

"So how do you tie this in with our discussion? If all this is so clear in the Scriptures, why do Christians deny what you say the Bible teaches?"

"I would suggest that the problem is not with those who don't believe it, *but with those who do*."

"How so?"

"Some Christians deny God's exhaustive sovereignty, and they live in a manner consistent with that denial. Other Christians affirm it, but then go on to deny it with their lives. The second group has more to answer for."

"You can't be saying that the church is in this sad condition because this is the way God has willed it?"

"Well, yes, I am. If God controls everything, then He certainly controls this."

"But *why*? That seems so contrary to everything I have ever learned about God and His relationship to the church."

"I don't know why either. I am not sure a creature could understand why. But I do know that I am not going to water down clear statements of Scripture just because I want to worship a God who meets with *my* approval!"

"Is there any passage of Scripture that teaches that God controls backslidings?"

"Yes. Isaiah 63:17. *O Lord, why have You made us stray from Your ways, and hardened our heart from Your fear? Return for Your servants' sake, the tribes of Your inheritance.*"

"So you are also saying that the reason so many Christians deny this truth is. . . ."

". . . is that God has willed it. Yes. He has hardened our hearts. And, anticipating the question, it does not lessen our responsibility in the slightest."

"Is it wrong to ask why God does this?"

"No. Isaiah asks why. I believe that when Christians acknowledge *that* God has done this, and begin tearfully asking *why* He has done it, we will be on the edge of true revival. True revival is something *He* gives."

I was shaking my head. "I don't know. . . ."

Martin went on. "The modern evangelical church is drowning in an ocean of theological stupidity. Here and there are handfuls of the 'orthodox' clinging to the wreckage of what was once a great ship. In such a condition, it is impertinent to even be tempted to pride."

"But why would God do that to His own ship?"

"He has done it, and He is God. That is enough. By all

that Scripture teaches, His reasons were good, just, and holy. And when we consider the glorious future that is promised for the gospel in the world, we should take courage as we pray for revival. It will be clear to us later."

"And in the meantime. . . ?"

"In the meantime, those Christians who have been given an understanding of this should not puff themselves up. We know that what Job says in Job 42:2 is true. *I know that You can do everything, and that no purpose of Yours can be withheld from You.* But they must also respond to this truth the way Job did in verses 5-6. *I have heard of You by the hearing of the ear, but now my eye sees You. Therefore I abhor myself, and repent in dust and ashes.*"

"How are you applying this?"

"It is one thing to hear truth, and agree with it. Many have come to believe these things simply because they are attracted to a *system* which is logically consistent. Or perhaps they are repelled by the shallowness of so much of our preaching and teaching today. Or they are the studious type, and like to read books by the Puritans."

Martin went on. "But it is quite *another* thing to be given a vision of the glory of God and to be, like Job, undone by it."

"Are you saying it is bad to be studious, or systematic?"

"No, not at all. Hard study is required by God, as well as to compare carefully one portion of Scripture with another. Over many years, many people have told me that I study too much, but the Holy Spirit convicts me regularly that I study too little."

"What are you saying then?"

"Hard study can be compared to chopping wood, assembling the kindling, and putting all the wood together for the fire. There are churches that have a good idea of where the wood should go, but they have forgotten there is supposed to be a fire."

"And others. . . ?"

"Others, theologically shallow, know there is supposed

to be a fire. But they use grass, thorns, paper, and a lot of lighter fluid."

"How do you see your work?"

"I have chopped a lot of good wood—although less than I should have—and I have assembled it. Now I am waiting, and praying to God."

"Praying for what?"

Martin thought for a moment.

"Praying for the fire to fall."

_____ eighteen _____

Systematics

"Is there a problem with approaching the Bible so systematically? When you answer my questions, you always seem to be consistent, and every answer fits in neatly with every other answer you give. It seems to me to be a tidy system. Is that correct?"

"Well, yes and no."

"Okay, explain."

Martin leaned back in his chair. "Why don't we start with you explaining what you mean by 'systematically.' Are you referring to systematic theology? In particular, my systematic theology?"

"Yes. Isn't systematic theology simply a Procrustean bed for the Bible? If a verse doesn't fit in with the system, then off with its head?"

"It can be, and frequently is. There are two major temptations when it comes to the study of systematics. The first is when the system is simply wrong and unbiblical, misleading the student of it as to the teaching of the Bible."

"Well, that is an obvious problem. What is the other?"

"The other can be a problem even when the system is correct. No, let me say it more strongly than that. *Especially* when the system is correct."

"What do you mean?"

"There is no way to talk about the Bible and what it contains without the speech being a summary of truth."

"All right. What does *that* mean?"

"Unless I read the whole Bible cover to cover every time I preach, or every time I share the gospel, or every time I answer a question, my speech necessarily has to be a summary of the contents of the Bible. It must be a systematic abstraction."

"Go on."

"Now I may either summarize poorly or well. But I cannot talk about the Word without summarizing. *That* is inescapable."

"Could you illustrate?"

"When Jesus says that loving God with all your heart, mind, strength, and soul is a summary of the Law and Prophets, He did so accurately. But suppose someone else said that the heart of the Law and Prophets was the verse about Og, King of Bashan having an iron bedstead. He would be inaccurate, to put it mildly."

"I see. Both statements are much shorter than the Bible, but one is an accurate condensation, and the other is not."

"Correct."

"So what is the problem with an accurate systematic?"

"The problem is the temptation to arrive at truth via a shortcut."

"Come again?"

"Systematic theology is like *Cliffs Notes*. If one has carefully read a book several times, say, *Pride and Prejudice*, the information in the notes can be a great help. But. . . ."

". . . there is a temptation to bypass reading the book, and content yourself with truth *about* the book."

"Exactly. And the more truth someone learns, the harder it is for him to see what he has done. But there are some who have seen this truth who have reacted into the opposite error."

"And what is that?"

"It is the error of thinking that systematic thinking and speaking about the Bible can be avoided. It cannot be. We have to choose between doing it poorly and doing it well. A refusal to think systematically about the Bible is, in the last analysis, a refusal to understand and apply. And that is basically a refusal to obey."

"I see. How would you relate this to our discussions on the sovereignty of God?"

"There are many Christians who agree with the things I have been telling you. Unfortunately, many of them have only read the *Cliffs Notes*. They subscribe to the Westminster Confession, for example, and they have never read their Bibles *once*."

"Okay."

"And then another group of Christians, who haven't read their Bibles either, rejects the teaching contained in *Cliffs Notes*. But the first group has made it easy for them. It is easy to reject the teaching of a work that is obviously the work of mere men."

"I get it. They can then throw it out in good conscience because it is merely the work of Calvin, or the Westminster divines."

"Right. But it is harder to throw out what Paul teaches in Romans, or John in his Gospel. If Christians would read their Bibles more, there would be a lot less controversy on the issue of God's exhaustive sovereignty. The Bible teaches it *plainly*."

"You are saying that if Christians read their Bibles more, they would become Reformed?"

"No. They would become *informed*," Martin grinned.

"I am still concerned that someone who is the adherent of a system will contradict the Bible for the sake of maintaining his system."

"It is a legitimate concern. Many have fallen prey to the temptation. But it is not a temptation that is limited to *formal* theological systems. Those who teach from the Bible informally can contradict the Scriptures, and themselves, just as readily. It is simply harder to catch them in it because they don't write big fat books with all their topics neatly arranged."

"So you are saying that it is not a question of whether

we hold a systematic theology or not. It is more a question of which systematic theology we will hold."

"Right. And all systematic theologies bring with them the temptation to set them over Scripture. The temptation is there always, whether the systematic is formal or informal, explicit or implicit, dry or slippery." Martin smiled.

"How should I proceed then?"

"Read your Bible. Again and again, over and over. As you read, listen to the teachers God has given to the Church. Some are alive, and speak to you as I do. Others are dead, but like Abel, still speak. Listen to them. Take what you hear back to Scripture again and again. As you do this, more and more truth will fall into place in your understanding."

"And how do I avoid the trap that goes with systematic study?"

"Never study theology apart from Bible reading. Read, read, and read some more. That will be ample protection."

I stood up. "Good night."

"Good night."

_____ nineteen _____

Hard Mercies

"Could you," I asked, settling into my chair, "tell me what brought you to these convictions? What started you on your study?"

Martin sat quietly for a moment, almost as if he were deciding whether or not to answer me. I hadn't realized I had asked him something personal. Finally, he spoke.

"I was in my last year of Bible school, and I was out one Saturday night. We were handing out tracts to the bar traffic. It had been an ordinary night in most respects. But around 9:30 I had an encounter with a man that changed my life.

"A middle-aged man with a gray beard came up and took a tract from me with some interest. He had a young bit of blonde fluff on his arm. She didn't say anything throughout the entire conversation. He didn't tell me what he did for a living, but I gathered that he was some kind of professor. He was certainly well-educated.

"He stood there, quietly reading the tract. When he was done, he handed it back to me, and then started to ask me questions. I have never been so mangled in debate in my life, before or since.

" 'I see here that you believe the Bible is the Word of God.'

" 'I certainly do,' I replied.

" 'Do you believe *all* of it?" he asked.

"I nodded, expecting a question about evolution, or

135

something like that. I was prepared in all the wrong places.

"He inclined his head toward his date.

" 'She and I are going to have a really good time later on. Do you think that's wrong?"

" 'That depends,' I said, 'on what you mean by "good time." '

"He laughed. 'We're spending the night together. Sleeping together. Making love. Having sex. You know. Do you think that's wrong?'

" 'Yes,' I said. I had never had a witnessing encounter like *this*.

" 'Why is it wrong?'

" 'Because,' I said, 'the Bible says it is wrong.'

" 'So,' he said, 'whatever the Bible says, you believe.'

" 'Yes,' I said.

" 'So,' he went on, 'you must believe that certain men are elected by God to salvation, and the others are hardened.'

"I was caught completely off guard. Our classes in Bible school rarely addressed the topic, and when they did it was in a cursory fashion. I remember being occasionally nervous about how some things were explained away, but I had trusted my instructors nevertheless.

" 'Well,' I said carefully, 'the Bible uses the word *election*. So I believe in it.'

"The man grinned, and took a drag on his cigarette. I could tell he thought he had bagged another one. I thought so too.

" 'What do *you* think the word means?' he asked.

" 'Different Bible scholars explain it differently.' I was floundering.

" 'Well, you are enough of a Bible scholar to tell me that sleeping with my friend here is sin. Surely you should know enough to tell me about this."

"I frankly didn't know what I thought. All I had was a vague prejudice against the exhaustive sovereignty of God. So I punted.

" 'God gave us free will. He foresaw what we would do with that free will, and He elected us on that basis.'

"The man's mocking grin grew broader. 'So! The Bible says that certain men are elected by God, and you, a fine Bible scholar, tell me it means certain men elect themselves! This is a fine hermeneutic, and I am in your debt for it! By this means, I need not feel any concern about the rest of my evening. The Bible says not to fornicate; this means I may fornicate as I please.'

"I had already turned red, and it occured to me that my only hope was to change the subject.

" 'You know the Bible fairly well, obviously. Why do you not believe it?'

"The man's eyes narrowed, and behind the outward good humor I could clearly see the hate. 'Because I know your Book well enough to know that the God of the Bible is a sovereign, all-controlling God. He is therefore a rival. I want to do as *I* please. *I* am sovereign.'

" 'But why do you want to fight with God?'

" 'The same reason you do. I don't believe the Bible because it is a threat to my autonomy. And *you* don't want your autonomy threatened any more than I do. The only difference between us is that you *pretend* to believe the Bible.'

" 'But this topic has been debated for centuries. Surely there are aspects that are not clear—'

"The man started to walk away. But then he turned and fired a parting shot. '*Therefore He has mercy on whom He wills, and whom He wills He hardens.* Those words are as clear as any in the Bible. If they are unclear, then the whole thing is unclear. I grew up in the church. I read my Bible. And the first time I saw those words I knew I hated them. Just like you.'

" 'I love this Book, and every word in it.'

"He wheeled around again. 'That's a truckload of crap and you know it. I hate the Christian God, but at least I know it. You hate Him, and pretend you don't. Next time try to learn your product before you go to sell it.'

"He disappeared, and I stood there crushed. I knew, I don't know how, that there was a lot of truth in his hateful words; he had really shaken me up. I went home right away, and that evening I started to study the Bible in a way that changed the course of my life. I resolved as I began the study that whatever God's Word revealed, I would believe and love. I was done fooling around. It wasn't but two months before I ran into real trouble at the Bible school, and almost didn't graduate. Maybe I'll tell you about that some other time."

Martin sat quietly for a moment. After the quiet started to weigh on me, I asked, "Have you ever met that man again?"

"No. I have prayed for him every day though. And I have prayed that I might meet him again. If God is merciful to me, it will happen."

"What about the girl he was with? Could you trace him through her?"

Martin smiled. "No. But she is a Christian now. She goes to that big church on the south of town. No. She doesn't remember his name."

"I have heard you refer before to *hard mercies*. Was this one?"

Martin nodded. "That," he said, "is exactly what it was."

_____ twenty _____

Conclusion

"So," I said, "can you put this all together for me?"

"You mean sort of an overview?"

"Exactly," I said.

Martin leaned forward in his chair, and motioned with his hands. "There are two basic pictures of man's state in the Bible. The first is that man is a *slave* to sin. The second is that man is *dead* in his transgressions and sins. In both cases, man is utterly helpless, and the helplessness is comprehensive. It affects everything he is, and everything he does."

"So the key is the helplessness of man. He cannot contribute to his own salvation?"

"Right. Man cannot lift himself out of the quagmire in which he finds himself. Like someone in quicksand, any 'advance' he makes in one area works to his disadvantage in another."

"What do you mean?"

"No part of him can work unaffected by the Fall. An unregenerate man (by himself) can desire salvation. He can truly want to go to Heaven when he dies. He can also understand what going to Heaven involves. *But he cannot do both at the same time.*"

"So you are saying that no natural man, understanding salvation, wants it."

"Correct. As Paul states, *no one* seeks after God. The sinful mind is hostile to God and cannot desire Him. But as

Paul also recognized, the unregenerate Jews did have a zeal for God, *but without knowledge*. This zeal only increased their condemnation. Paul, before his conversion, delighted in the law of God, and had a great zeal for it. But he also hated the people of God."

"I think I have gotten confused here. You are saying that no one seeks after God, and yet some people have a zeal for God?"

"A zeal *without knowledge*. Seeking after God on your own terms, with your own understanding, is simply a subtle way of running from Him."

"Check."

"An unregenerate man can love the Word of God, but only so long as he misunderstands it. An unregenerate man can understand the Word of God, but only so long as he hates it."

"I see what you mean by a quagmire. If he *lifts* his arm, the rest of him *sinks* deeper."

"You've got it. The sinful mind is hostile to God. This does not mean that the non-Christian cannot praise God or pray to Him. It does mean that everything is done in the context of his larger rebellion against God. And the context affects everything. Therefore, when he praises God, even his praise is sin. When he prays, his prayer is an offense. This means that evangelical obedience, obeying the gospel, is impossible for the non-Christian. He cannot repent properly, and he cannot believe properly. He can perform what he believes to be repentance (but which is actually a worldly sorrow unto death), and he can assent to the truths of the Christian religion. But as he does these things, he will always be doing something else that negates or denies it. He will take back with one hand what he gives with the other. He cannot remove himself from the context of his rebellion. He cannot cease rebelling; he cannot surrender. If he runs up the white flag, it is with treachery in his heart."

"All right. You have told me about the works of men,

and the condemnation we have earned for ourselves. What about the work of God?"

"Do you mind a triune answer?"

I smiled. "No, and what do you mean?"

"You asked about the work of God. Let's begin with the work of the Father, and then go on to the work of the Son and Holy Spirit."

"Fine."

"Election is the work of the Father. Before the world was formed, before time began, the Father chose certain individuals for salvation from their sins, and gave those individuals as a gift to the Son. Those whom He chose not to elect, by definition, He passed by."

"Why?"

"Because it was His sovereign pleasure to do so. Because He is light, and in Him is no darkness at all. That should be enough to satisfy us."

"All right. Go on."

"In a world where there are distinctions between individuals, those distinctions must be God-ordained. Otherwise God is not *God* at all. Election is a truth that can be seen merely by looking around us. Before I was convinced of the truth of election as God revealed it in the Bible, I began to see it in the world around me in God's natural revelation. Why was I born into a Christian family, surrounded by love and the gospel? The day I was born, thousands of others were born far away from this position of spiritual privilege. Why was I brought up in a way that lead to my salvation? Why was I not born into a Christless family, surrounded by nothing but superstition and sin? Why did I not die when I was seven back in a jungle somewhere with flies on my face? Why was I born so spiritually privileged?"

I nodded. I had often felt the same sense of undeserved privilege. Martin continued.

"Nothing is clearer than the fact that God placed me into the family He did, and that He only put three children there. Why wasn't it four, with one less given to a family lost in sin? Does not God have control over such things?"

"But couldn't it be said in response that all these blessings, however great, were all external? You could still have
rejected Christ in spite of them, couldn't you?"

"Well, let's grant that for the sake of discussion. We are
just talking about external blessings; we cannot see in natural revelation the full biblical doctrine of election. But external blessings, when they concern the physical presence of
those who know and teach the gospel, are not irrelevant. We
can see that God does not treat every man alike, and that
the distinctions He makes have *some* bearing on who is saved,
and who not. In order to deny this, someone would have to
say that there is no correlation between how much the gospel is preached, and how many people are saved."

"I see. You are saying that when it comes to *access* to
saving truth, God does not treat all men the same."

"Exactly. And this is a truth which no evangelical Christian can consistently deny."

"All right. Is there anything else you saw in this external
blessing?"

"Well, it was also clear that this decision to place me in
a godly family was made before I had done anything, good or
bad. In other words, there is no way to be proud over things
such as this. What do I have that I did not receive? And if I
received it, how can I boast as though I did not? Under God's
government of the world, there are clear distinctions made
between individuals which pertain to salvation. Now if a certain measure of election can be seen in natural revelation,
we should not be surprised to find it clearly spelled out in the
Bible. And this is exactly what we find. We have already
discussed the passages which teach this."

"So the next thing would be the work of the Son on the
cross?"

"Yes. The Son of God purchased a people for Himself
out of the slave market of sin. His redemption was particular
and definite."

"He had something in mind when He died?"

"Right. The Son came to earth, not to do His own will, but rather the will of the Father. Jesus was not seeking to accomplish anything more than what the Father had decreed."

"I see. You are saying that if Jesus died with the intention of saving anyone who was not chosen by the Father, then He was no longer seeking to do the will of the Father."

"Yes. Let us say that Jones has died without Christ, and that he has gone to his judgment. With him now in Hell, is it possible to say that God *secured* salvation for him through the cross?"

"No. When God secures something, it is secure."

"So then, the real question is whether God has *secured* anything through the cross. The teaching of the Bible is that He secured salvation for His people. Those who differ with this must therefore say that in the cross, God secured a *potential* salvation."

"What about the universal passages. . . those where it says God loved the world, and that sort of thing?"

"God does love the world. He sent His Son to die for the world, and take its sin away."

"So you believe that the world is elect, and that the gospel will one day be triumphant?"

"Yes."

"And that the world will be saved, although not every last individual will be saved."

"You've got it."

"So what is the work of the Spirit?"

"We are born again by the work of the Spirit. I mentioned earlier that we were dead in our sins. It is the Spirit who resurrects us to new life. He brings to fruition the choice of the Father, and the purchase of the Son. The Father chooses, the Son purchases, and the Spirit regenerates."

"So this brings us to the issue that first brought me here. Can a Christian lose his salvation?"

"Consider it this way. A man is dead in his sin. But before the world was created, the Father chose him for salvation. On the basis of this choice, the Son came two thousand years ago and laid down His life to purchase this man from the slave market of sin. On the basis of *this*, the Holy Spirit regenerated him two years ago. Now, what makes us think that this particular work of God is capable of being interrupted and frustrated? It cannot be. If salvation is a work of man, sure, we could lose it. We lose lots of things. But if it is the work of God, then the work shall stand, and it will stand for eternity."

"Amen," I said, and got up to go. "I guess I'll see you on Sunday."